# Pier Fishing on San Francisco Bay

THE COMPLETE FISHING GUIDE TO PUBLIC PIERS AROUND SAN FRANCISCO BAY

## Mike Hayden

Chronicle Books  /  San Francisco

**Library of Congress Cataloging in Publication Data**
Hayden, Mike.
    Pier fishing on San Francisco Bay.

1. Saltwater fishing—California—San Francisco Bay.
2. Fishing—California—San Francisco Bay.
3. Piers—California—San Francisco Bay. I. Title.
SH473.H39         799.1'66632              81-3799
ISBN 0-87701-138-9                         AACR2

Typography by Communi-Comp
Cover photo by Hal Lauritzen
Cartography by Milne

CHRONICLE BOOKS
870 Market Street
San Francisco, CA 94102

# Contents

## East Bay Piers

## North Bay Piers

## Ocean Piers

# Introduction to Pier Fishing I

For people who live in the San Francisco Bay Area, saltwater pier fishing involves less time, effort, and expense than any other kind of angling. A state license is not required to fish Bay and coastal waters from a public pier. No advance reservations are needed, and access to all but a few privately operated piers is free. Besides tackle, the only requisite is bait and perhaps a box lunch.

Bait and tackle shops abound on both sides of the Bay. Most of the larger piers adjoin a snack bar, restaurant, or waterfront park with picnic facilities.

Tackle as uncomplicated as an ordinary hand line may be used on piers to catch a variety of perch and the delectable starry flounder. The basic know-how is easily learned. For this reason, fishing piers are especially popular with families that have small children. For the same reason, piers are made to order for the casual angler whose skills may be a little rusty.

Also the public piers are patronized by many fishermen of the dyed-in-the-wool kind who come equipped to tangle with a striped bass or monster white sturgeon. Surveys of marine angling indicate that skiff fishermen catch three times as many fish per day as fishermen on piers. However, this finding is based on a statistical average. It doesn't allow for the days when boat trips must be scrubbed because of rough water.

The principal advantage enjoyed by skiff fishermen is mobility. They can prospect the Bay until they discover where the fish are feeding. But not infrequently, the fish are found concentrated directly off a pier. This is because the pilings of piers provide a habitat for mussels, marine worms, and various kinds of crustaceans. These edibles attract small fish which, in turn, attract big fish.

When fishing is slow, the piers accommodate diversions such as backgammon, boat watching, or listening to a sportscast, which help pass the time until the action picks up. There are days when the fish bite only at a certain stage of the tide. Some of the best pier fishing on the Bay occurs after dark. Several piers located on the East Bay are equipped with lights for night fishing.

Twenty years ago, public fishing piers were a novelty on San Francisco Bay. Less than a dozen miles of the Bay's 276-mile shoreline were open to fishing or other recreation. The water was too polluted for swimming. The Bay was rapidly dwindling in size as tidelands were filled for housing and commercial development.

The present proliferation of fishing piers, waterfront parks, wildlife refuges, and small-boat launching sites on the Bay began with a simple idea. The idea was that a great natural harbor, endowed with many kinds of fish and a beautiful mountain setting, should be preserved and made accessible to the people who lived near its shores.

A ground swell of support for this idea in the late 1950's eventually resulted in new legislation and government-funded programs to rehabilitate the Bay. In 1957, California's Wildlife Conservation Board launched a pier fishing program by renovating a portion of the decaying Berkeley Pier. A small fishing pier was built from scratch at San Leandro in 1963. About this time, the pier program gained impetus from a Fish and Game Department survey of saltwater angling in the northern part of the state.

Among other things, the survey showed that pier and shore fishing are more popular than boat fishing, notwithstanding the fact that boat fishermen catch more fish. This finding probably surprised nobody, in view of how convenient it is to fish from a pier. But the survey helped justify the allocation of millions of dollars to provide more public piers on the Bay.

Of the thirty-odd piers listed in this book, nine were constructed by the Wildlife Conservation Board during the 1970's. Half the cost was paid for by the town or county that agreed to operate and maintain the pier after it was built. The rest came from state horse racing revenues, several bond acts, and a number of federal grants, including California's share of an excise tax on fishing tackle.

Several fishing piers on the Oakland and San Francisco waterfronts were entirely funded and built by the port authorities. But much of the credit for these piers belongs to the Bay Conservation and Development Commission. The legislation that created this agency in 1965 provides that no bay-fill be permitted other than for water-oriented purposes in the public interest.

Approval by the Bay Conservation and Development Commission is required for any bay-fill or extensive shoreline development. If a permit is granted, the law requires that public access to the Bay be provided to the maximum extent possible. So when port authorities negotiated for a permit to build a new terminal on San Francisco's southern waterfront, they agreed to build Agua Vista Park and equip it with a fishing pier. Port View Park, with its attractive lighted pier, was a trade-off for filling the site

of the old Oakland Mole and replacing it with container facilities.

Access to the Bay has improved in recent years to the extent that ninety miles of shoreline have become available for recreation and nature study. Long stretches of waterfront have been acquired for the Golden Gate National Recreation Area and a number of state and regional parks. Most of these parks include one or more fishing piers.

Of great significance to the sport fishery has been the establishment of National Wildlife Refuges on San Pablo Bay and the South Bay. The salt marshes in these preserves are vital to the food supply of fish. The marsh plants help maintain the water quality by recycling nitrates and phosphates contained in the discharges of sewage treatment plants.

Strengthening of the state pollution laws and construction of modern treatment plants has brought about a dramatic improvement in the water quality of the Bay. The bacteria count is down to the extent that swimming is now permitted off most Bay beaches. Marine biologists engaged in a study for the Regional Water Quality Board are optimistic their findings may lead to a resumption of oyster farming.

In a separate study, Fish and Game Department researchers are analyzing Bay clams to detect the presence of such industrial pollutants as heavy metals, pesticides, and petroleum products. Should traces of a contaminant be found, it will not necessarily mean the clams are unfit for consumption. The whole question of permissible standards for toxic substances is fraught with controversy in scientific circles.

For example, specimens of striped bass taken from the Bay have been found to contain methyl mercury in amounts above the maximum permitted by the U.S. Food and Drug Administration for interstate commerce. State health officials advise against eating more than one meal a week of a striped bass that weighs four pounds or more. But some scientists say mercury in any quantity is harmful. It may be cold comfort for the angler who chooses to consume his catch that mercury compounds derived from pesticides or processing may turn up in fruits, vegetables, and meats.

The law requires that all toxic wastes be treated before discharge into the Bay. But just any common substance, such as sugar, salt, or sawdust, may be destructive to fishlife if present in sufficient concentrations. Most kinds of fish would be long gone from the Bay were it not for the flushing action of ocean tides and the inflow of water from the Sacramento-San Joaquin River Delta.

The dark cloud hanging over the Bay fishery emanates from the Delta, which drains half of California. Here a vast amount of runoff which used to pass out the Golden Gate is now diverted to agribusiness and cities in the southern part of the state. The water leaves the southern edge of the Delta by way of the California Aqueduct and the federal government's Delta-Mendota Canal. Each year, millions of baby striped bass are drawn into these waterways at tremendous cost to the fishery. Elaborate fish screens installed at the intakes of the pumping stations are not effective in preventing the loss of juvenile bass.

Now the state plans to boost the amount of water sent south by excavating an enormous ditch which would bypass the Delta. It would deliver water from the Sacramento River directly to the pumping stations. This would reduce the loss of fish in the southern part of the Delta but create a similar problem in the north. It would mean far less water to dilute and flush out pollutants from the Bay and Delta. Also critics say it would allow saltwater to infiltrate the Delta to the detriment of local industry and agriculture, as well as fishlife.

Public fishing piers will become expensive anachronisms if the Bay is permitted to regress to its former status as a glorified cesspool. However, opposition to the Peripheral Canal appears to be growing stronger, while the project is stalled pending a statewide referendum. Locally active on the issue is the Save San Francisco Bay Association which sparked the campaign to curb bay-fill and improve public access. Below are several organizations with a special interest in the ecology of the Bay.

- Audubon Society, 2718 Telegraph Avenue, Berkeley (415) 843-2222
- Oceanic Society, Bay Chapter, Fort Mason, San Francisco (415) 441-5970
- Save San Francisco Bay Association, P.O. Box 925, Berkeley 94701

## CALIFORNIA FISH AND GAME PUBLICATIONS

Ocean Fishing Map of San Francisco, San Mateo, and Santa Cruz Counties
Guide to the Coastal Marine Fishes of California, Fish Bulletin 157, 1972
Common Ocean Fishes of the California Coast, Fish Bulletin 91, 1953
Life History of the Starry Flounder, Fish Bulletin 79, 1950
Fish and Wildlife Resources of the San Francisco Bay Area, Water Projects Branch Report No. 1, 1962
Fish and Game Department booklets— "Inshore Fishes of California," "Offshore Fishes of California," "Anadromous Fishes of California," and "Marine Baits of California"

For price list of Fish and Game publications currently available, write:
Publications Section
Box 1015
North Highlands, California 95660

For subscription to bimonthly magazine, OUTDOOR CALIFORNIA, mail two dollars ($2.00) with request to the Publications Section, Box 1015, North Highlands, California 95660.

6

# Bait and Tackle for Pier Fishing II

Most kinds of saltwater angling, such as surf casting or deep trolling, call for tackle that meets fairly exact specifications. An angler who attempted to surf cast with a five-foot boat rod would place himself at a serious disadvantage. Conversely, a fourteen-foot surf rod would be nigh impossible to handle on a rockfish party-boat. Part of the charm of pier fishing is that most any conventional tackle may be used to catch fish.

However, there is no one combination of rod and reel that is suitable for taking all the different kinds of fish found off piers. Also the choice of tackle may depend as much on water conditions as on the species of fish the angler hopes to catch.

For example, the array of tackle seen on weekends at Pacifica Pier includes everything from dinky freshwater spinning outfits to Calcutta surf rods of impressive dimensions. The spinning gear is great for hooking small perch when water conditions permit use of a few split shot for weight. A massive Calcutta rod is no fun at all for catching perch of any size. But it would be a better choice than light spinning gear should water conditions require use of a heavy sinker.

Some of the regulars at Pacifica bring as many as five rod and reel combinations to the pier and fish with two at one time (the legal limit). Typically, one rod is used for bottom fishing. The other is rigged with a bobber to take fish that are feeding closer to the surface.

### ROD AND REEL

When selecting a rod for pier fishing, it helps to keep in mind all the functions this item of tackle is expected to perform. The rod should enable the angler to cast, feel a bite, and set the hook. It should be flexible enough to act as a shock absorber while permitting the angler to maintain a taut line until the fish is exhausted.

Probably the closest thing to all-purpose tackle for pier fishing is a saltwater spinning outfit that some manufacturers specify for "light surf, pier, and jetty fishing." Such a rod may measure eight to nine feet from butt to tip. It should have a sensitive tip but enough backbone to cast a four-ounce sinker. An important consideration for the angler who uses public transportation is that the rod breaks down into two sections.

A fairly rugged open-faced spinning reel with a smooth operating drag is preferred by the regulars. The reel should match the rod and accommodate at least 200 yards of fifteen-pound test monofilament line.

### TERMINAL TACKLE

The main items of terminal tackle used in pier fishing are snaps, swivels, hooks, leaders, and sinkers. The lore of pier fishing as regards terminal tackle is vast. All sorts of rigs are

For bottom fishing results, try this terminal rig: two snelled hooks looped to a swiveled leader weighted with a pyramid sinker.

employed by the regulars depending on the bait used, the fish sought, and the water conditions off the pier. However, the most widely used rig for bottom fishing is easy to assemble provided a ready-made bass leader is used. These leaders come in various breaking strengths and are available at most bait stores.

The swivel at one end of the leader is attached to the main line. A swivel-snap at the other end is used to engage the sinker. There are two dropper loops on the leader to accommodate a pair of snelled hooks.

A snelled hook has a short piece of line fastened to the shank with a loop at the end for securing the hook to the leader. Snelled hooks in a wide range of sizes may be obtained at bait and tackle shops.

Many types of lead sinkers are used on the piers. Some of the regulars use old spark plugs. The main idea is to select the lightest sinker that will take the bait to the bottom. A pyramid sinker is the most versatile of weights. The wire loop at the flat end of this sinker is attached to the leader when the sinker is used to anchor the bait in one spot. But should the angler wish to keep the bait in motion with a slow retrieve, then the loop at the pointed end of the sinker should be fastened to the leader.

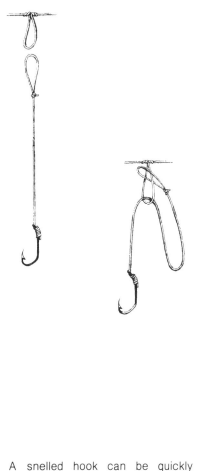

A snelled hook can be quickly attached to (or detached from) a simple loop knot in the leader.

The sliding sinker rig is often effective for catching flounder, especially where there is enough current to keep the bait in motion. The sliding sinker is threaded on the main line and kept from sliding down to the hook by a swivel interposed between the main line and the leader. When a twitch of the rod tip signals that a flounder may be sampling the bait, the sliding sinker permits the angler to pay out line so that the fish feels no resistance before it decides the bait is safe to eat.

No leader is required when fishing with light tackle near the surface for topsmelt, jacksmelt, or shiner perch. A single hook may be attached to the end of the main line with a few split shot clamped to the line a foot or so above the hook. Bobbers are commonly used to maintain the bait at the depth where fish are hitting.

ACCESSORIES

In place of a tackle box, a small knapsack with several pockets may be used to bring spare tackle, including swivels, snaps, leaders, hooks, and a variety of sinkers in assorted sizes.

Some sort of measuring device is required should the catch include crabs or any fish that is subject to a minimum size limit. A popular

item available at most bait and tackle stores is a small fish scale that contains a tape measure.

The surest way to know when a fish is nibbling the bait is to hand hold the rod. But when the action is slow, the rod may be rested against the pier railing with a small bell attached to the rod tip. Bells with a spring clip or other fastening device may be obtained at most bait shops located near the waterfront. Some of the regulars use a rod holder that clamps to the pier railing.

Depending on facilities at the pier, a bait board may not be needed but a sharp knife is essential for cutting bait and dressing the catch. Another useful item is a scaler with saw teeth. It does the job of removing fish scales better than a knife. An old piece of towelling comes in handy after handling bait or fish.

Useful for trimming frayed line and disgorging hooks from the catch is a pair of needlenosed pliers with a cutting edge.

BAIT

The northern anchovy is the fish most widely used for cut bait on piers. Fresh caught anchovies make the best bait but are rarely available at bait stores. In the Bay Area, most anchovy bait is sold as fresh-frozen.

Anchovies may be used as chunk bait or strip bait. To prepare as strip bait, the fish are scaled and filleted. The fillets are then cut lengthwise or crosswise into strips of the desired size.

After scaling, chunk bait is prepared by slicing the fish crosswise through the backbone into chunks about an inch wide. Chunk bait is mainly used by anglers fishing for striped bass. The hook is thrust through the back side of the chunk, then turned and brought down so the point penetrates the lower side.

Other cut baits sold by bait stores include clams, prawns, and squid. Sometimes, herring and Pacific sardine (a great bait for stripers) are available.

Good live baits for perch are shore crabs and pile worms. Shore crabs about the size of a penny may be gathered along stony flats exposed at low tide. These are baited by inserting the hook up through the underside near the hind legs.

Pile worms are native to the Coast and a staple item at bait stores. But sometimes the demand is such that the worms must be flown in from the East Coast. Blood worms are effective as bait but a Fish and Game Department publication warns that these creatures have jaws that can deliver "a nasty venomous bite."

Another name for grass shrimp is bay shrimp. This crustacean and the ghost shrimp may appeal to flounder and striped bass, as well as sturgeon. Some bait shops carry both kinds of shrimp but, at times, the supply is limited. Grass shrimp may be hooked in the head or tail. A popular method is to insert the hook down through the head and then turn the point up into the tail to conceal the barb.

The little fish most commonly used as live bait for stripers are the shiner perch, northern anchovy, long-jawed mudsucker, and the staghorn sculpin or bullhead. Any of these may tempt a striper depending on what "old linesides" happens to be feeding on. Mudsuckers may be available at some bait stores but the other species are easiest to obtain by fishing for them with hook and line. The fish are usually rigged for live bait fishing by inserting the hook through the lower jaw and snout.

# BAIT SHOPS

**El Granada**
Pillar Point Bait and Tackle, Pillar Point Harbor (415) 728-5675

**Half Moon Bay**
Hilltop Grocery & Fishing Supplies, 251 San Mateo Road (415) 726-4950

**Pacifica**
Coastside No. 2 Bait and Tackle, 1604 Francisco Boulevard (415) 355-9901
Pacifica Fishing Pier, Pacifica (tackle rented) (415) 355-7437
Pacifica Sports Center, 2130 Palmetto Avenue (415) 355-7437

**San Bruno**
Peninsula Sea Food Mart, 135 El Camino Real (415) 589-0532

**San Francisco**
Dave Sullivan's Sport Shop, 5323 Geary Boulevard (415) 751-7070
Luie's Bait and Tackle Shop, 195 Broad Street (415) 586-5347
Mission Rock Resort, 817 China Basin (415) 621-5538
Modern Bait & Tackle Shop, 2975 Mission (415) 824-5450
Muny Bait & Sport Shop, 3098 Polk Street (tackle rented) (415) 673-9815
Red's Bayview Bait & Tackle, 4408 Third Street (415) 282-3242
Slim's Bait & Tackle Shop, 5256 Third Street (415) 822-2494
The Ramp, 855 China Basin (415) 621-2378
Wong's Bait & Tackle Shop, 1630 Post (415) 563-9819

**San Mateo**
Shor-Vu Hardware, 530 South Norfolk Street (415) 344-9413
Sun Valley Store, 620 South Norfolk Street (415) 343-4690

**Benicia**
The Tackle Shop, 523 West J Street · (707) 745-4921

**Martinez**
Bill's Bait and Payless Gas, 835 Alhambra Avenue · (415) 229-3150
Depot Bait, 400A Ferry Street · (415) 228-2203
Open Bait & Tackle Shop, 11 North Court Street · (415) 229-3220

**Richmond**
Baroni's Bait & Tackle Shop, 960 Thirteenth Street · (415) 233-5028
Johnson Brothers Bait, 111 West Cutting Boulevard · (415) 235-5335
Point San Pablo Bait & Tackle, Point San Pablo Yacht Harbor · (415) 233-7132
Red Rock Bait Shop, Red Rock Marina · (415) 234-1058

**Rodeo**
Old Sarge Bait & Tackle, Foot of Pacific Avenue (tackle rented) · (415) 799-4076
Rodeo Bait Shop, 603 Parker Avenue · (415) 799-2641

**San Pablo**
Long's Bait Shop, 14600 San Pablo Avenue · (415) 234-2388

**Vallejo**
J & M Market, 900 Sonoma Boulevard · (707) 642-6920
Joe's Bait Shop, 1305 Sonoma Boulevard · (707) 642-1096
Napa-Val Fishing Resort, P. O. Box 549, Napa River at Sears Point Road · (707) 642-3984
The Pier, Sears Point Bridge and Wilson Avenue · (707) 642-4330

## EAST BAY

**Alameda**
Central Ave. Bait & Tackle Shop, 641 Central Avenue · (415) 522-6731
Grand Street Bait & Tackle Shop, 1926 Grand Street · (415) 521-2460

**Berkeley**

| | |
|---|---|
| BBB Liquors, 1050 Gillman | (415) 524-0572 |
| Berkeley Bait & Tackle, 1479 San Pablo Avenue | (415) 526-5830 |
| Berkeley Marina Sport Center, 225 University Avenue | (415) 849-2727 |

**Emeryville**

| | |
|---|---|
| Hank Schramm's Sport Fishing Center, 3310 Powell (tackle rented) | (415) 654-6040 |

**Oakland**

| | |
|---|---|
| Captain Scotty's Bait & Tackle, Dock & Spice Box, 87 Jack London Square | (415) 832-0119 |
| Lee Anderson's Bait, Tackle & Fish Shop, 6702 San Pablo Avenue | (415) 428-9514 |
| Lew Bait & Tackle, 1624 East Fourteenth | (415) 534-1131 |
| Lucky Bait Shop, 6608 San Pablo Avenue | (415) 652-3316 |
| Monterey Bait, 4715 East Fourteenth Street | (415) 261-5562 |
| Oyster Pirates, Park View Park, Foot of Seventh Street | (415) 465-2764 |
| Pacific Bait & Tackle Shop, 6334 San Pablo Avenue | (415) 652-7102 |
| Robbie's Bait Shop, 7704 East Fourteenth Street | (415) 638-1006 |

**San Leandro**

| | |
|---|---|
| Ron's Tackle Sales, 293 MacArthur Boulevard | (415) 632-3200 |

MARIN

**Sausalito**

| | |
|---|---|
| Caruso's Sportfishing, Foot of Harbor Boulevard | (415) 332-1015 |
| Meatball Bait Distributors, Marinship | (415) 332-2281 |
| Sausalito Boat & Tackle Shop, Waldo Point | (415) 332-2599 |
| Sunbeam Bait Co., 1702 Bridgeway | (415) 332-2842 |

**San Rafael**

| | |
|---|---|
| Loch Lomond Live Bait House, Dock A, Loch Lomond Yacht Harbor | (415) 456-0321 |

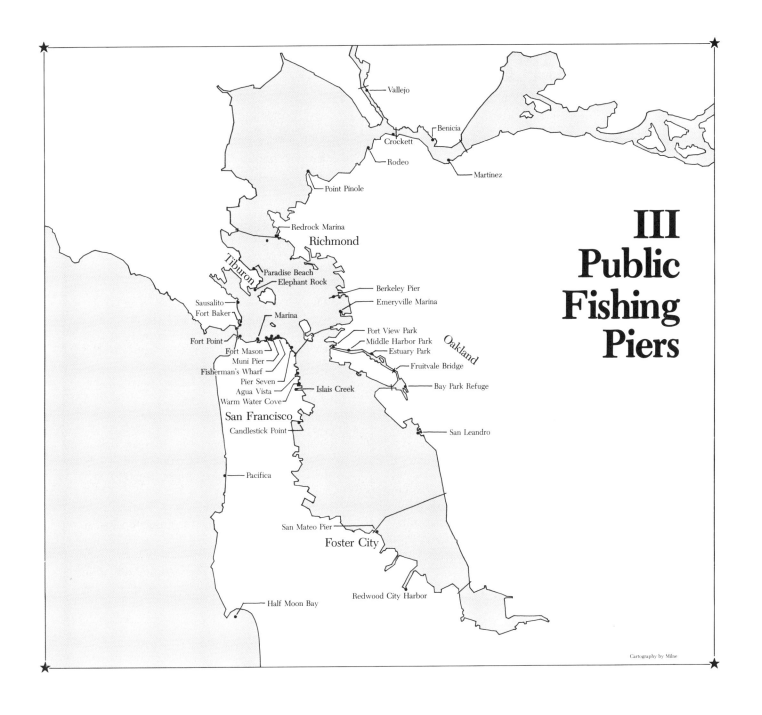

Vallejo

Benicia

Crockett

Rodeo

Martinez

Point Pinole

Redrock Marina

Richmond

Tiburon

Paradise Beach
Elephant Rock

Berkeley Pier

Emeryville Marina

Sausalito
Fort Baker

Marina

Port View Park
Middle Harbor Park
Estuary Park

Oakland

Fort Point

Fort Mason
Muni Pier
Fisherman's Wharf
Pier Seven
Agua Vista
Warm Water Cove

Islais Creek

Fruitvale Bridge

Bay Park Refuge

San Francisco

Candlestick Point

San Leandro

Pacifica

San Mateo Pier

Foster City

Redwood City Harbor

Half Moon Bay

# III
# Public
# Fishing
# Piers

Cartography by Milne

# 1. Fort Point

On a slender, wave-battered shelf below serpentine cliffs and the South Tower of the Golden Gate Bridge stands a fort from another century with gun ports, casemates, and walls of brick and granite 36 feet thick. More often than not wreathed in coastal fog, Fort Point provides a dramatic setting for a fishing excursion. Both the Fort Point Pier and the sea wall that rims the road to the fort afford excellent fishing at times.

The pier is an old wharf once used by the navy to stevedore mines. Flounder, perch, and a variety of other fish are caught here but the pier is best known as a rewarding place to trap red rock crabs.

Species of fish rarely caught from piers inside the Golden Gate may be hooked off the sea wall near the fort. These include monkeyface eels, cabezone, and greenling sea trout.

Eighty feet above the present fort, the Spanish built a fortress in the 1790's known as El Castillo de San Joaquin. It had fallen into disrepair by the time Fremont emplaced guns here during the Bear Flag Revolt. Fort Point was completed in 1861 and was garrisoned with two companies of artillerymen who never found an enemy on whom to train the fort's 126 cannon. The fort was declared obsolete in 1905 and dedicated in 1971 as the first National Park site in the Bay Area.

LOCATION:
Underneath the South Tower of the Golden Gate Bridge at the foot of Marine Drive.

HOW TO GET THERE:
*Auto:* From Lincoln Avenue, turn off on Long Avenue and proceed to Marine Drive.
*Public Transportation:* Take a Golden Gate Transit Bus or San Francisco Municipal Railway Bus No. 28 (Nineteenth Avenue) to the Golden Gate Bridge toll plaza. Leave the plaza by way of the path that begins north of the Joseph Strauss statue.

FACILITIES:
Rest rooms near entrance to the fort. Admission to the fort is free. Tours conducted daily. Fort opens at 10:00 A.M. and closes at 5:00 P.M.

HOURS:
Fishing pier is closed from sunset to sunrise.

ADMINISTRATION:
Golden Gate National Recreation Area, a unit of the National Park Sevice. Headquarters are located at Fort Mason, Bay and Franklin

streets, San Francisco. The Fort Point Administrative Office is situated near the foot of the Fort Point Pier. For information, call (415) 556-1693.

NOTE:
Striped bass fishing with bait or lures is sometimes red hot at the sea wall but as at other shore fishing locations on the Bay, it's strictly a hit or miss proposition. By the time news of the action is reported in the sports pages of the newspaper, the bass are likely to have moved to another part of the Bay.

A waterfront route for hikers and joggers, known as the Golden Gate Promenade, runs 3½ miles from Fort Point to Aquatic Park. There are numerous places to shore fish on the stretch between the Fort and the Marina Green.

Beneath the Golden Gate, a fisherman tries to lure a rockfish from the submerged ledge off the Fort Point sea wall.

# 2. Marina Green

The Marina Green is a flat expanse of green grass and small boat moorage which stretches just short of a mile between Fort Mason and a military post at Crissy Field. No fishing piers are situated here. However, the catwalk at Gas House Cove and the outer seawall east of the St. Francis Yacht Club provide much the same kind of fishing and facilities as a proper pier.

The Marina was formerly a large cove on the bay. It was filled to provide a site for the 1915 Panama Pacific International Exposition, held to celebrate the opening of the Panama Canal. The Tower of Jewels, the Court of the Universe —all the fair buildings are gone except the Palace of Fine Arts which fronts a duck pond off Baker Street.

LOCATION:
Off Marina Boulevard between Crissy Field and Fort Mason in San Francisco.

HOW TO GET THERE:
*Auto:* From the Golden Gate Bridge by way of Doyle Drive. From Lombard Street (US 101) by way of Bay or Fillmore streets.
*Public Transportation:* San Francisco Municipal Railway Bus No. 22 (Fillmore) runs to Marina Boulevard at the Marina Green. Bus No. 30 (Stockton) runs to Beach Street, two blocks from the Green.

FACILITIES:
Snack shop, drinking fountain, and rest rooms.

HOURS:
Pier open 24 hours, daily.

**ADMINISTRATION:**
Golden Gate National Recreation Area, a unit of the National Park Service. Headquarters at Fort Mason, Bay and Franklin streets, San Francisco (415) 566-0560.

**NOTE:**
A state angling license is required to fish off the Marina Seawall and the catwalk at Gas House Cove.

# 3. Fort Mason

A first-time visitor to Fort Mason looking for a spot to fish off the old Army docks might well wonder what this waterfront is all about. Since the fort was acquired in 1972 as headquarters for the 43,790-acre Golden Gate National Recreation Area, the nine large buildings in the dock area have been put to a bewildering number of uses. More than forty nonprofit groups lease space here from the Fort Mason Foundation for diverse cultural, educational, and recreational activities. In 1980, two of the covered piers were used to house a trade fair sponsored by the Peoples Republic of China.

Only ticket holders were permitted on the piers during the China fair which drew tens of thousands of visitors. However, except during such special events, much of the waterfront is available for sport fishing.

Pier 1 has been set aside as a maintenance yard for the Park Service. A Liberty ship from World War II is moored on one side of Pier 3. The opposite side and all of Pier 2 are open to fishermen. Flounder, perch, kingfish, tomcod, smelt, sharks, striped bass, and, on rare occasions, a salmon are caught off the piers. Crabbing for red rock crabs is often productive off the far end of Pier 2.

Up the hill that rises behind the dock area are wooded picnic areas. Picnic sites with tables, benches and grills are located near the former site of a Spanish cannon installed in 1797 to protect an anchorage east of Black Point. Fort Mason served as a troop transport center from 1892 until 1962, when the Army moved its transport operations to Oakland. Over a million soldiers embarked from Fort Mason in World War II.

LOCATION:
Main entrance is located at the intersection of Bay and Franklin streets in San Francisco.

HOW TO GET THERE:
*Auto:* Entrance to parking space on the Fort Mason waterfront is located at the intersection of Marina Boulevard and Buchanan Street. From the Golden Gate Bridge, proceed east on Doyle Drive to Marina Boulevard. From San Francisco Civic Center, follow US 101 by way of Van Ness Avenue and Lombard Street to Fillmore Street. Turn right on Fillmore and then right on Marina Boulevard.
*Public Transportation:* San Francisco Municipal Railway Bus No. 28 (Nineteenth Avenue) runs to Bay and Laguna streets, two blocks from the entrance to the dock area. Bus No. 30 (Stockton) and No. 47 (Potrero) stop near the intersection of Van Ness Avenue and Bay Street, one block from the main entrance to the fort.

FACILITIES:
Rest rooms are located near the entrance to the dock parking area on the Marina Green. Vegetarian meals served in dock area at Zen Center Greens Restaurant. Picnic areas located up the hill behind the dock area. Brochure describing park facilities and points of interest available at headquarters of the GGNRA in Building No. 308 near the main entrance.

HOURS:
Piers are open to fishing during daylight hours.

ADMINISTRATION:
Golden Gate National Recreation Area (GGNRA), a unit of the National Park Service. The Superintendent's office is located at Fort Mason in Building No. 308. For general park information, call (415) 556-0560. For update on activities in the dock area (theatre productions, art exhibits, concerts, festivals, field trips, classes in boat building and marine ecology), call (415) 441-5705.

# 4. Muni Pier

An easy stroll from Fisherman's Wharf and the boutiques of Ghirardelli Square is the little cove at Aquatic Park where square-rigged vessels anchored during the Spanish occupation. Here, a circular concrete jetty, 1,850 feet in length, protects the cove and serves as a public fishing pier. It is still listed as the San Francisco Municipal Pier and spoken of affectionately as the Muni Pier although everything at Aquatic Park is now federal property, administered since 1977 as part of the Golden Gate National Recreation Area.

Aquatic Park is a legacy of the former Works Progress Administration that was created to provide employment during the depression years of the 1930's. After the cove was dredged of debris accumulated from the 1906 earthquake, the WPA crews constructed a triple-decked "people's palace" intended to serve as a bathhouse and social center. The building was designed to resemble the superstructure of a contemporary battleship. Now this striking version of Art Moderne houses the National Maritime Museum.

The Muni Pier was completed several years before Aquatic Park was officially dedicated in 1939. Although the pier shows signs of aging and lacks the refinements of newer facilities, it retains its popularity as a fishing spot and as a great place to watch the traffic of cargo vessels, sailing yachts, and diverse small craft on the Bay.

Perch and kingfish account for a preponderance of the catch most days in summer. Striped bass are taken mainly in late summer and early autumn. February through early March seems to be the prime time at Muni Pier to fish for Pacific tomcod. This small fish, which rarely grows longer than a foot in length, is the only true cod that abounds in California waters. The so-called rock cods taken in large numbers by sport fishing party boats belong to the rockfish family *Scorpaenidea*.

Tomcod are regarded by some anglers as a nuisance but esteemed by many old hands as a superior table fish. One of the regulars at the Muni Pier compares the flavor and eating quality of tomcod with that of rainbow trout. He recommends fishing from the midsection of the pier with light tackle, a half-ounce sinker, and No. 6 or No. 8 hook baited with a pile worm, shrimp, or slice of anchovy.

At the foot of the Muni Pier, a shorter pier angles out toward Black Point. Formerly known as Transport Wharf No. 4, it was the landing for a steamer that served the prison on Alcatraz Island. Now it's a popular spot for trapping red rock crabs.

LOCATION:
Foot of Van Ness Avenue between Fort Mason and Fisherman's Wharf, San Francisco.

HOW TO GET THERE:
*Auto:* Drive to the foot of Van Ness Avenue.
*Public Transportation:* San Francisco Municipal Railway Bus No. 19 (Polk), No. 30 (Stockton), No. 32 (Embarcadero), and No. 47 (Potrero). No. 42 (Downtown Loop) runs to Fisherman's Wharf and touches bases at the Transbay Terminal and Southern Pacific Railway Station. No. 15 (Third Street) runs to Northpoint and Taylor which is two blocks from Fisherman's Wharf.

FACILITIES:
Snack shop, drinking fountain, and rest rooms located near the pier. Choice of benches, bleachers, and green lawn for a picnic. Attractions include the National Maritime Museum and the Hyde Street Wharf (admission fifty cents) where a number of antique vessels are berthed, including the steam schooner *Wapama* and the walking beam ferry *Eureka.* Hours are 10:00 A.M. to 5:00 P.M. A senior center is located at the east end of the National Maritime Museum building. Hours are 9:00 A.M. to 4:00 P.M.

HOURS:
Pier open 24 hours, daily.

ADMINISTRATION:
Golden Gate National Recreation Area, a unit of the National Park Service. Headquarters are located at Fort Mason inside the main entrance at Bay and Franklin streets. For information, call (415) 556-0560.

NOTE:
The Muni Pier is buffeted by strong breezes most afternoons. When it gets too windy, some anglers go over to Fort Mason where the lee side of Pier 2 provides a sheltered spot to fish. The dock area may be approached on a road reserved for pedestrians that leaves Aquatic Park near the foot of Muni Pier.

Greenling seatrout and several species of rockfish frequent the rockfill which provides a foundation for the Muni Pier. According to a publication of the State Fish and Game Department, over forty different species of fish have been identified in the sport catch at the pier.

# 5. Pier Seven

Pier Seven at the foot of Broadway is one of several piers located north of the Ferry Building where no cargo or passenger ship has docked for years. Some pier sheds have been converted to offices for lawyers and architects. Pier 39, once a berth for tramp steamers, is now a tourist-oriented esplanade of boutiques and theme restaurants. But poor old Pier Seven, its transit shed destroyed by fire in 1973, appears destined to spend the rest of its days as a parking lot for commuters.

The far end of this spacious, 800-foot-long pier is reserved for fishing. Here anglers may bottom fish in water 35 feet deep while contemplating the movement of vessels off Treasure Island. An occasional striped bass and many perch, kingfish, and skates are caught off the pier in summer.

LOCATION:
Off the Embarcadero at the foot of Broadway.

HOW TO GET THERE:
*Auto:* By way of the Embarcadero.
*Public Transportation:* San Francisco Municipal Railway Bus No. 32 (Embarcadero) runs from Fourth and Townsend (Southern Pacific Railway Station) to Fisherman's Wharf and Aquatic Park.

FACILITIES:
Just the pier. It's a short walk to restaurants located on the Embarcadero between Piers Seven and Nine and in the vicinity of the Ferry Building.

HOURS:
Pier open during daylight hours, daily.

ADMINISTRATION:
Metropolitan Parking Corporation, 525 Mission Street, San Francisco 94105 (415) 928-2700

A waterfront panorama seen from the Ferry Building along the Embarcadero does not distract this hook-baiting fisherman on Pier Seven.

# 6. Fisherman's Wharf Area

From Pier 39 west to Aquatic Park, the San Francisco waterfront is occupied by a colorful array of restaurants, shopping malls, and tourist-oriented attractions. Trans-Pacific steamers no longer call here. Maritime activity is confined to commercial fishing craft and the cruise boats that feature trips to Alcatraz and tours around the Bay.

The possibilities for angling begin at the foot of Grant Avenue. Here Pier 39 groans under the weight of a spanking new double-decked pavilion filled with 132 business enterprises. These include ice cream parlors, souvenir stands, a penny arcade, scores of specialty shops, and a wide choice of places to eat. Not the least controversial aspect of Pier 39 is the all-of-a-kind architecture, described by one critic as "Cannery Shed Moderne."

A platform at the far end of Pier 39 provides fishing in water 35 feet deep. It is the best spot on the waterfront to view Alcatraz Island. But a less congested place to cast a bait is the new pier signed Public Shore which adjoins the marina west of the pavilion. This long open pier is equipped with lighting to accommodate night fishing.

From Pier 39, it's a short walk to the heart of the Fisherman's Wharf area which takes in Pier 45 and two boat basins where most of the city's commercial fishing fleet is based. The uncovered docks which rim and intersect the basins are largely open to the public. Some with access to fishable water are furnished with benches. But, however interesting, Fisherman's Wharf is neither the most productive nor relaxing place to wet a line, especially on weekends when the area swarms with visitors.

LOCATION:
The Embarcadero from the foot of Grant Avenue to Taylor Street and Jefferson Street from Taylor to Hyde Street.

HOW TO GET THERE:
*Auto:* From the San Francisco Skyway (Interstate 80), take the Embarcadero Freeway (State 480) to Battery Street. Drive one block west to Sansome Street by way of Broadway and proceed north to the Embarcadero.
*Public Transportation:* San Francisco Municipal Railway cable car No. 59 or Powell-Hyde cable car No. 60 and buses No. 19 (Polk), No. 32 (Embarcadero), No. 15 (Third), and No. 42 (Downtown Loop).

FACILITIES:
Public rest rooms at Pier 39 and near Shed A at Pier 45.

HOURS:
Pier open 24 hours, daily.

ADMINISTRATION:
Port of San Francisco, Ferry Building, San Francisco (415) 391-8000. Pier 39, The Embarcadero, San Francisco (415) 981-8030.

# 7. Agua Vista

PIER FISHING ON SAN FRANCISCO BAY

Agua Vista is a neat little park situated south of the Bay Bridge in the old maritime district served by China Basin Street. Now highly industrialized and crisscrossed with railway tracks, this waterfront once provided a placid mooring for hay scows, whaling ships, and a large fleet of Chinese shrimp boats.

Just thirty feet wide, Agua Vista occupies a nicely landscaped strip of frontage on the Central Basin. The main attraction is a short T-shaped pier where anglers may watch the traffic of pleasure boats from nearby marinas while waiting for a fish to bite. The pier provides a good view of the Bethlehem Shipyard. The huge facility was established in the 1880's by the Union Iron Company, San Francisco's first heavy industry.

Perch, flounder, and an occasional striper are caught at the pier. When wind becomes a problem, it's a short walk south on China Basin Street to a more sheltered spot to fish at the foot of Mariposa Street. Here, close by the Ramp Marina, a walkway is signed Public

Viewing Area. The path leads to a small piece of shore which adjoins the marina's boat ramp.

LOCATION
China Basin Street between Pier 64 and Mission Rock Resort.

HOW TO GET THERE
*Auto:* By way of Third Street to intersection with China Basin Street.
*Public Transportation:* To intersection of Third and Mariposa streets on San Francisco Municipal Railway Bus No. 15 (Third Street).

FACILITIES
A thousand square feet of pier. Picnic tables with benches. Rest rooms, public phone, bait shop, and a restaurant overlooking the waterfront are at adjoining Mission Rock Resort, 817 China Basin Street. Bait sold at The Ramp, 855 China Basin Street.

HOURS
Pier open 24 hours, daily.

ADMINISTRATION
Port of San Francisco, Ferry Building, San Francisco 94111 (415) 391-8000.

A busy shipyard and marina does not seem to bother the fishing at the Port of San Francisco's popular Agua Vista Park.

# 8. Warm Water Cove

One of the most obscure, least likely fishing spots on the San Francisco waterfront is a small wooden pier situated at the outlet of a steam power plant on Warm Water Cove. Access is by way of a path that leads down from the foot of 24th Street. There are few improvements at the cove other than the pier and some benches. But despite the drab industrial setting and lack of amenities, Warm Water Cove is popular with fishermen, especially on windy days.

Nothing is more certain to rob pier fishing of its charm than chill, damp blasts of marine air from an unrelenting west wind. Warm Water Cove enjoys a devoted following among the regulars because it stays flat calm even when the prevailing wind whips most of the Bay into a froth of whitecaps.

It's not unusual for a whole school of striped bass to enter the cove on a foraging expedition. When this happens, an expertly presented streamer fly may take as many fish as bait. One reason the cove attracts perch, flounder, and stripers relates to the operation of the steam plant. It seems the water that is drawn from the Bay for cooling purposes and then discharged into the cove carries with it a variety of natural fish foods.

The steam plant was built around the turn of the century by the sugar magnate, Claus Spreckels. It was one of the few powerhouses in San Francisco to escape destruction by the 1906 earthquake.

LOCATION:
Foot of 24th Street.

HOW TO GET THERE:
*Auto:* From Third Street, drive east on 23rd Street, turn right on Illinois Street and proceed a short block to 24th Street.
*Public Transportation:* To intersection of Third and 23rd streets on San Francisco Municipal Railway Bus No. 15 (Third Street).

FACILITIES:
Small T-shaped pier, benches, portable-type chemical toilets.

HOURS:
Pier open 24 hours, daily.

ADMINISTRATION:
Port of San Francisco, Ferry Building, San Francisco 94111 (415) 391-8000.

NOTES:
Fishing is apt to be poor at Warm Water Cove during low stages of the tide.

Starry flounder, one of the tastiest of all the catches from Bay Area piers, bite best during the winter and early spring.

# 9. Islais Creek

On San Francisco's southern waterfront near the produce district, Third Street crosses a ship channel known as Islais Creek. Upstream from the six-lane drawbridge are the copra docks of the Cargill Company. Downstream are petroleum docks, a wharf where tallow is shipped to the Orient, a huge container facility capable of handling nine vessels at one time, and the Port of San Francisco's grain terminal which can load ships at the rate of 1,200 tons an hour.

Easily overlooked in this maritime setting are two obscure little parks where anglers with a state license may fish the channel. These mini-parks are located on opposite sides of the waterway off the east side of Third Street.

The name Islais is derived from the word Islay which is an Indian name for the holly-leaved cherry. The ship channel is the only visible remnant of a stream which once originated on San Francisco's Twin Peaks.

LOCATION:
Third Street two blocks from Army Street.

HOW TO GET THERE:
*Auto:* Leave US 101 Bayshore Freeway at Third Street exit.
*Public Transportation:* San Francisco Municipal Railway Bus No. 15 (Third Street).

FACILITIES:
Benches and tables.

HOURS:
Pier open 24 hours, daily.

ADMINISTRATION:
Port of San Francisco, Ferry Building, San Francisco (415) 391-8000.

NOTES:
Before the parks at the Third Street crossing of Islais Creek were established, there were no guard rails at these locations. What can happen when guard rails are absent is illustrated by this item which appeared in the *San Francisco News* February 21, 1958, under the headline, "BIG FISH DROWNS ANGLER IN THE BAY:"

> A youth who went to the aid of another angler was pulled into the Bay by a big fish and drowned yesterday. Carl D. Sigler, 19, of 1271 Hudson Ave., was asked by Mrs. Dorethey Antoine, 55, of 565 Fell St., to help her land the fish when she had trouble after a big 'strike' at Pier 92 on Islais Creek.
>
> She said Sigler was playing out the line when the fish—presumably a leopard shark—lunged and pulled him into the water. The Coast Guard recovered his body.

Striped bass school out in the ocean, but they pass within striking distance of some Bay piers on their autumn migration into the Delta.

# 10. Candlestick Point

For years, the San Francisco waterfront across the road from Candlestick Park where the Giants and Forty Niners play was an ugly dumping round. There was no public access but, every winter, fishermen would pick their way through the debris to approach the shoreline of Candlestick Point. It would have taken more than No Trespassing signs to stop them because the tidal flats off the point provide some of the best flounder fishing on the South Bay.

Presently, a 170-acre California State Recreation Area is being created on Candlestick Point. It will eventually take in four miles of shoreline between Hunters Point and the San Mateo County Line. The first 22-acre unit with parking and picnic facilities was opened to the public in 1979.

An old pier south of the stadium has been rebuilt. Windbreaks have been installed along the west shore of the point for the benefit of bank fishermen. When rehabilitation of the east shore is completed and all the greenery that has been planted becomes established, Candlestick Point promises to be one of the most attractive waterfront parks inside the Golden Gate.

Candlestick Point is unique as the first inner city state park in the Bay Area. It adjoins the Bayview-Hunters Point district where parkland and waterfront access are in short supply. Much credit for the new park goes to Hunters Point community leaders who waged a thirteen-year campaign for funding of a recreation area at Candlestick.

Anglers who regularly fish from the pier at Candlestick say it's not unusual at low tide to spot a large skate cruising the shallows for shellfish. It's fascinating to watch one of these creatures employ its pectoral fins to glide through the water much as a bird uses its wings to soar through the air. Mussels, which make excellent bait, abound in the shallows alongside the pier. A screwdriver may be used to pry these shellfish from rocks exposed at low tide.

LOCATION:
Off the Hunters Point Expressway opposite Candlestick Park in San Francisco.

HOW TO GET THERE:
*Auto:* Southbound from San Francisco, leave 101 Freeway at Third Street exit and follow signs to vicinity of Candlestick Park. Northbound from San Mateo, take Harney Street exit.

*Public Transportation:* No regularly scheduled bus service. Both SamTrans and the San Fran-

The old pier at new Candlestick Point State Recreation Area offers some of the best shore fishing along the Peninsula side of the Bay.

cisco Municipal Railway run special buses to the stadium on days that games are scheduled.

## FACILITIES:
Benches and table for cutting bait and dressing fish on the pier. Good parking a short piece up the road inside the main entrance to the state recreation area. Nearby are rest rooms and picnic facilities shielded by windbreaks.

## HOURS:
Pier open 24 hours, daily.

## ADMINISTRATION:
California Department of Parks and Recreation, Box 2390, Sacramento 95814 (916) 445-6477. For information on Candlestick Point State Recreation Area, call (415) 822-9266.

## NOTES:
Historians provide at least two explanations for the origin of the name Candlestick. Gladys Hansen, San Francisco City Archivist and author of the *San Francisco Almanac*, writes, "Sometime prior to 1910, the shoreline in this area was quite irregular with mud and shallow water adjacent to it. Before filling operations began to extend the shoreline outward, there existed a land form in the shape of a candelabra. This form has now disappeared."

Erwin G. Gudde in *California Place Names* writes, "In 1894, the Coast Survey established a triangulation station here and named it after Candlestick Rock, an eight-foot sharp pinnacle shown on the map of the Board of Tide Land Commissioners, 1869. The extreme eastern part of the stadium structure marks the approximate location of the pinnacle."

# 11. San Mateo Pier

The longest fishing pier on San Francisco Bay stretches 4,135 feet from Foster City's waterfront to the main ship channel on the South Bay. Anglers who hike to the far end of this San Mateo County facility may fish water forty feet deep. Also known as the Foster City Pier or Werder Wharf, the pier was reconstructed in 1972 from a remnant of the old San Mateo-Hayward drawbridge.

The quality of fishing off the San Mateo Pier tends to run to extremes. When the regulars say it's good, it's apt to be very good for perch, smelt, or flounder. When they say it's slow, it means people here are catching nothing but undersized sharks. When they say it's bad, it is safe to assume not even the bullheads are biting. But whatever the prognosis, a patient angler at the San Mateo Pier always stands a chance of hooking a fair-sized halibut or striped bass. The most impressive catch reported in 1980 was a 121-pound white sturgeon hooked on a "slow" day in March.

Considering the long walk back to shore, it was a stroke of good planning for the rest rooms to be situated at the halfway mark on the pier. Unhappily, these facilities were recently wrecked by vandals. When this book went to press, there was talk the pier might be leased to a concessionaire but no spokesperson for the county would confirm this.

LOCATION:
Foster City waterfront on the south side of the San Mateo-Hayward Bridge.

HOW TO GET THERE:
*Auto:* Leave US 101 Bayshore Freeway at the Hillsdale exit and drive east by way of Hillsdale Boulevard and Beach Park Boulevard to the pier.
*Public Transportation:* SamTrans Bus No. 44C from Hillsdale Shopping Center stops at Crane and Pelican, about six blocks from the pier.

FACILITIES:
None other than parking until facilities damaged by vandals are repaired.

HOURS:
A sign at the entrance to parking area indicates the pier closes at dark but many anglers fish here at night.

ADMINISTRATION:
San Mateo County Parks and Recreation Department, County Office Building, Redwood City (415) 364-5600.

A ring net is one way to prevent your prize catch from breaking free of the hook while lifting it onto the pier.

# 12. Redwood City Harbor

The port of Redwood City is the only deep water port on the South Bay. It specializes in handling bulk cargos such as scrap iron, salt, lumber, cement, and petroleum. The public fishing pier leans out a few feet on this busy harbor at the Redwood City Municipal Marina. It's not unheard of for a fair-sized striped bass to be hooked here. However, the pier is mainly of interest to young people who enjoy catching bullheads, small perch, and baby sharks.

Presently, no public fishing piers are located on the Bay south of Redwood City. A catwalk at Palo Alto Yacht Harbor leads to a platform on salt marsh that is flooded at high tide. This facility serves as an observation post for bird watchers and is located too far inshore to provide good fishing. Perhaps as early as 1982 after the new Dumbarton Bridge is completed, a section of the old span will become available for fishing.

LOCATION:
451 Harbor Boulevard, Redwood City.

HOW TO GET THERE:
*Auto:* From US 101 Bayshore Freeway, take Harbor Boulevard to the Redwood City Municipal Marina. The turnoff is marked by a Charley Brown's Restaurant sign.

*Public Transportation:* None.

FACILITIES:
Tap water at pier. Soft drink machine, public phone, and rest rooms at the Harbormaster's Office.

HOURS:
Pier open 24 hours, daily.

ADMINISTRATION:
Redwood City Parks and Recreation Department, 1400 Roosevelt, Redwood City (415) 364-6060.

Two happy young anglers display their catch.

# 13. San Leandro

PIER FISHING ON SAN FRANCISCO BAY

San Leandro's elegant 475-berth marina is sheltered by two fingers of land which are nicely landscaped and maintained as parks. A small T-shaped pier fronts the channel off the south finger. Perch, flounder, striped bass, and skates may be hooked here but usually sharks provide most of the catch.

The marina is part of the 1,600-acre San Leandro Shoreline Recreation Area. Presently, there are no fishing piers on the Alameda County shore south of San Leandro. However, at least two piers are in the planning stage on the South Bay. When the new Dumbarton Bridge is completed in 1981, portions of the old span on opposing sides of the Bay will be retained as fishing piers.

LOCATION:
San Leandro, foot of Marina Drive.

HOW TO GET THERE:
*Auto:* From Highway 17, proceed west on Marina Drive, turn left on Neptune Drive and then right on the South Dike Road.

A deck-chaired fisherman takes his afternoon leisure on the public fishing pier at attractive San Leandro Shoreline Recreation Area.

*Public Transportation:* AC Transit Bus No. 55. This bus connects with the San Leandro BART Station.

FACILITIES:
Drinking fountain, rest rooms, tree-shaded picnic areas with benches, tables, and grills. Two restaurants near the Marina. Close by is Marina Park which includes a lagoon and a large children's play area.

HOURS
Pier open 24 hours, daily.

ADMINISTRATION:
San Leandro Recreation Department, 835 East 14th Street, San Leandro (415) 577-3462. For information on the pier and other facilities, call the Harbormaster's Office (415) 577-3472.

# 14. Bay Park Refuge

When this book was printed, the Bay Park Refuge on San Leandro Bay was closed to the public. It is expected to reopen early in 1981 with completion of new picnic facilities and a bicycle path. However, present plans call for repair of the park fishing pier and also construction of a new pier which will be approached on a walkway through Arrowhead Marsh. Neither facility may be available for fishing before late 1981.

Bay Park Refuge was made a bird sanctuary by the state in 1931. Birds which frequent the marshes here include plovers, terns, avocets, black-necked stilts, horned larks, western grebes, snowy egrets, and great blue herons.

LOCATION:
South of Alameda Island and due west of the Oakland Coliseum.

HOW TO GET THERE:
*Auto:* From the Nimitz Freeway (Highway 17), take Hegenberger Road to Edgewater Drive. Park entrance lies at the end of Edgewater.
*Public Transportation:* AC Transit Bus No. 57 (Hegenberger Road-Bart Coliseum). Operates during commute hours only.

42

FACILITIES:
See remarks above.

ADMINISTRATION:
East Bay Regional Park District, 11500 Skyline Boulevard, Oakland 94619. For parks information, call (415) 531-9300.

Black-necked stilts are among the many kinds of shore birds that are the pier fisherman's frequent companions out on the tidal flats.

# 15. Fruitvale Bridge

The Fruitvale Bridge is a drawbridge of the bascule type. It spans a man-made ship channel which links the Oakland Estuary with San Leandro Bay. Alameda Island was a peninsula before this waterway was completed in 1902.

When the present Fruitvale Bridge was built in the 1970's to replace an obsolete span, the Army Engineers installed platforms for fishermen at both ends of the bridge. Since then, the bridge has become a popular place for night fishing.

Mostly striped bass are taken from the small pier on the Alameda side of the channel. Here, the current is swifter than off the larger Oakland pier where perch, as well as bass, may be hooked. In July of 1980, stripers to forty pounds were reported caught at the bridge by anglers using live shiner perch as bait.

LOCATION:
Alameda Pier: Foot of Versailles Avenue in Alameda. Oakland Pier: Off Alameda Avenue near intersection with Fruitvale Avenue in Oakland.

HOW TO GET THERE:
*Auto:* Take Nimitz Freeway (Highway 17) to the Fruitvale Avenue exit.

*Public Transportation:* AC Transit Buses Nos. 33A, 58, and O stop near the intersection of Fernside Boulevard and Versailles Avenue. From here, walk three blocks on Versailles to the bridge. The O bus runs to San Francisco. Bus 33 connects with BART's Twelfth Street Station but operates only during commute hours.

FACILITIES:
Oakland Pier: Benches.
Alameda Pier: Benches and lighting.

HOURS:
Oakland Pier: Open 24 hours, daily.
Alameda Pier: Closed from 9:00 P.M. to 7:00 A.M.

ADMINISTRATION:
Oakland Pier: Oakland Parks and Recreation Department, 1520 Lakeside Drive, Oakland (415) 273-3091. Alameda Pier: Alameda Recreation and Park Department, Santa Clara Avenue and Oak Street, Alameda (415) 522-4100.

Matching piers at either end of the Fruitvale Bridge are favorite spots to try for striped bass on long-lingering summer twilights.

NOTICE
THE FISHING PIER,
DECK, PLATFORM, AND
ENTRY WAY ARE
CLOSED TO PUBLIC USE
9 P.M. TO 7 A.M.

# 16. Estuary Park

Estuary Park is an attractive city park of 7½ acres bound on two sides by fishable water. It's located at the confluence of the Oakland Estuary with a tidal channel that is signed on old charts as San Antonio Creek.

Under Mexican rule, the Oakland Estuary was known as the Estero de San Antonio. In 1907, one-half mile upstream from the estuary, San Antonio Creek was impounded to create 160-acre Lake Merritt. This saltwater lagoon in the heart of downtown Oakland is the oldest wildlife sanctuary in the United States.

The small fishing pier at Estuary Park extends a few feet onto the estuary over water 15 feet deep. Here and from the quay on the tidal channel, young people fish for perch and kingfish. Now and then, a striped bass is hooked. The park includes a boat launching ramp and picnic facilities shaded by poplar trees.

LOCATION:
On Oakland's Embarcadero, eight blocks east of Jack London Square.

HOW TO GET THERE:
*Auto:* Leave Nimitz Freeway (Highway 17) at Jackson Street exit. Drive south on Jackson,

The parklike setting at Estuary Park
fishing pier in Oakland is also convenient
to the restaurants and shops of Jack
London Square.

Three young fishermen along Estuary
Park quayside test the tidal slough that
drains Lake Merritt into the Estuary.

turn left on the Embarcadero, and proceed
four blocks to the park.
*Public Transportation:* AC Transit Buses Nos. 32,
33A, and 36.

FACILITIES:
Drinking fountain, benches, tables, and rest
rooms. Bait shop and choice of restaurants at
Jack London Square.

HOURS:
Pier open 24 hours, daily.

ADMINISTRATION:
Oakland Parks and Recreation Department,
1520 Lakeside Drive, Oakland (415) 273-3091.

# 17. Middle Harbor Park

About the last place anyone might expect to find a park on the Oakland Estuary is the highly industrialized waterfront at Middle Harbor. Yet here, alongside the huge container docks of the United States Lines, is Middle Harbor Park, a sliver of green lawn adorned with some trees and shrubs. The most prominent feature of this well-maintained park is a small fishing pier. Kingfish, perch, and striped bass may be hooked off the pier, which is one of the best places on the estuary for boat watching.

LOCATION:
Middle Harbor at the foot of Ferro Street in Oakland.

HOW TO GET THERE:
*Auto:* From Nimitz Freeway (Highway 17), drive south on Adeline Street which runs into Middle Harbor Road. Follow Middle Harbor Road to the United States Lines Terminal. Turn left to cross the tracks here and then right on Moorship Avenue. Ferro Street leads off to the waterfront at the west end of the terminal.
*Public Transportation:* None.

FACILITIES:
Benches, tables, drinking fountain. Water tap at the pier.

HOURS:
Pier open 24 hours, daily.

ADMINISTRATION:
Port of Oakland, 66 Jack London Square, Oakland (415) 444-3188.

Redtail surfperch bite all year from piers around the South Bay shore, but the big redtail bite best in winter and early spring.

EAST BAY PIERS

# 18. Port View Park

The octagonal-shaped fishing pier at Port View Park is a favorite spot on the East Bay for night fishing. Over a hundred striped bass have been reported caught from this lighted pier on a single evening. There's also good bank fishing at Port View, which occupies 2½ acres next door to the Seventh Street Marine Terminal. The park and terminal share the tip of a man-made peninsula which juts out on San Francisco Bay from the Port of Oakland's Outer Harbor.

Before the peninsula was built in the late 1960's, the waterfront began off Seventh Street near the former Albers Brothers Milling plant that is now occupied by the Carnation Company. From here, the famous Oakland Mole bore the tracks of the Southern Pacific Railroad to a ferry slip two miles out on the bay. Transcontinental trains were met here by ferryboats from 1869 through the spring of 1959.

First-time visitors are likely to be impressed by the number of massive container yards seen on the drive to Port View Park by way of Maritime and Seventh streets. As of 1980, Oakland could boast the largest container port on the West Coast. It overtook the Port of San Francisco primarily because it could provide more space for container storage.

Port View Park is imaginatively landscaped with evergreen shrubs and a bizarre observation tower that rises four stories tall. The fishing pier has a well in the center where anglers may drop their lines when the water off the pier is too rough or the outer rail is too crowded with fishermen. Other than bass, the catch includes kingfish, rubberlip perch, flounder, halibut, sharks, and skates. Often, brown pelicans may be observed off the pier executing their fantastic power dives for fish.

LOCATION:
Foot of Seventh Street, Oakland.

HOW TO GET THERE:
*Auto:* Driving from San Francisco by way of the Bay Bridge, leave Interstate 80 at the West Grand Avenue exit and shortly thereafter leave West Grand at the Harbor Terminals exit. Proceed south on Maritime Street to Seventh Street. From Nimitz Freeway (Highway 17), take the Eighth Street exit and proceed west to Peralta. Turn left on Peralta and then right on Seventh Street.
*Public Transportation:* AC Transit Bus No. 83M operates during commute hours only.

FACILITIES:
Benches, lighting on the pier. Benches and
tables with charcoal grills, drinking fountain,
rest rooms, observation tower, and snack shop
with bait sales.

HOURS:
Pier open 24 hours, daily.

ADMINISTRATION:
Port of Oakland, 66 Jack London Square,
Oakland (415) 444-3188.

EAST BAY PIERS

51

# 19. Emeryville Marina

San Franciscans who haven't kept up with the East Bay may find it easier to believe there are cows in Berkeley than a public fishing pier at Emeryville.

In the Gay Nineties, Emeryville was a place to have fun, the site of fairs, circuses, festivals, and horse races. But early in this century when horse racing was banned, the village became a no-nonsense factory town, bereft of a church, theater, or municipal park. Then, in the 1970's, plush restaurants and condominiums sprang up across the East Shore Freeway on an artificial peninsula which now shelters a modern marina.

A well-equipped fishing pier with lighting was completed at the marina in 1979. Because this pier enjoys the protection of the harbor, it offers a pleasant alternative to Berkeley Pier on windy afternoons. Flounder, kingfish, and rubberlip perch are some of the fish caught here in significant numbers.

LOCATION:
Foot of Powell Street, Emeryville.

HOW TO GET THERE:
*Auto:* Leave Interstate 80 East Shore Freeway at Emeryville exit.

FACILITIES:
Seats, lighting, water taps, and fish cleaning racks on the pier. Rest rooms, picnic area with benches and tables, fish market with bait and tackle sales, choice of restaurants.

HOURS:
Pier open 24 hours, daily.

ADMINISTRATION:
City of Emeryville, 2449 Powell, Emeryville (415) 654-6161. Marina (415) 658-8732.

The newest fishing pier on the Bay is at the Emeryville Marina. Flounder, kingfish, and rubberlip perch are common catches here.

# 20. Berkeley Pier

By sunrise on summer weekends, all the choice spots to wet a line at Berkeley Pier are apt to be taken. Anglers long on patience and know-how catch striped bass here to 45 pounds. But the pier is also popular as a place to take small children on their first fishing expedition.

Even when angling is slow at the pier for most kinds of fish, either bullheads or shiner perch are likely to furnish all the action a very young person could want. These little fish may be hooked on scraps of cut bait with a simple hand line or light freshwater tackle. Family outings are best confined to the morning hours because the pier is buffeted by a stiff breeze most afternoons.

Berkeley Pier is part of a 131-acre recreation area which includes several restaurants, a wooded park with picnic tables and winding nature paths, and an 800-berth yacht harbor. Since Gold Rush days, the site has provided a boat mooring, beginning with a makeshift wharf for produce and lumber schooners. Here, in the 1920's, the Golden Gate Ferry Company built the longest pier on the Bay.

To reach water more than ten feet deep for a ferry landing, it was necessary to run the pier to a point 3½ miles from shore. Ferry service ended and the City of Berkeley took over the pier with the completion of the San Francisco-Oakland Bay Bridge in 1936.

A San Francisco guidebook published in 1940 lists "The Berkeley Municipal Fishing Pier (fee 5¢)." But it seems much of the aging structure was posted off limits to the public by World War II. In 1959, two thousand linear feet of the old pier were rehabilitated as a fishing platform with funds partly supplied by the California Wildlife Conservation Board. An additional thousand feet of renovated pier was added in 1962.

Aside from bullheads (staghorn sculpins), the fish most commonly caught at Berkeley Pier are kingfish, smelt, flounder, skates, sharks, and a variety of perch. Most sought after by adult fishermen are halibut and striped bass.

LOCATION:
Foot of University Avenue.

HOW TO GET THERE:
*Auto:* From East Shore Freeway (Interstate 80), take the University Avenue exit.
*Public Transportation:* AC Transit Line Bus No. 51 M runs to the pier.

**FACILITIES:**
Fish cleaning racks, rest rooms, overhead lighting, and benches (some with windbreaks and charcoal grills). Within easy walking distance are several restaurants, a bait shop, and Shorebird Park.

**HOURS:**
Pier open 24 hours, daily.

**ADMINISTRATION:**
City of Berkeley Marina Sports Center
University Avenue, Berkeley (415) 849-2727.

# 21. Red Rock Marina

After the most controversial bridge on the Bay displaced the Richmond-San Rafael Ferry in 1956, the ferry landing at Castro Point was developed as a fishing resort and marina. Shelter for small craft was provided by sinking a string of old barges that were filled with rock. The largest wharf was made to serve as a public fishing pier for which a modest fee was charged.

For some years, the Red Rock Marina was a popular fishing spot, notwithstanding its obscure location in an industrial area occupied by several refineries and petroleum docks. But recently, most of the fishing pier was fenced off and posted for use as a commercial fish landing.

The small portion of the wharf that remains open to the public (at no charge) sometimes affords excellent angling for perch. Filled as it is with old pilings, derelict barges, and decaying ferry slips, the harbor is attractive to fish looking for food and shelter.

Red Rock Marina was named for a rocky isle, rich in iron oxides. It rises 169 feet above the water about a mile off Castro Point, south of the Richmond-San Rafael Bridge. The latter span is unique on the Bay as the only bridge that is lower in the middle than at both ends. Red Rock was formerly named Golden Rock because it was believed to contain treasure buried by pirates.

LOCATION:
The Richmond Shore at Castro Point north of the Richmond-San Rafael Bridge.

HOW TO GET THERE:
*Auto:* Driving west on Highway 17, take Point Molate exit which is located near the toll plaza of the Richmond-San Rafael Bridge. A short distance north of the freeway, the road forks three ways. The left fork leads to the marina.
*Public Transportation:* None.

A sunken barge, old pilings, and decaying ferry slips provide refuge and good forage for perch at the Red Rock Marina pier.

EAST BAY PIERS

# 22. Point Pinole

Point Pinole Regional Shoreline, which first opened to the public in 1973, is one of the largest waterfront parks in the Bay Area. It takes in 2,147 acres of pebbly beach, salt marsh, grassy meadows, and eucalyptus forest on a peninsula where the Hercules Powder Company used to manufacture dynamite and other explosives. Few traces of the factories remain. The park is managed as a natural area where no vehicles other than the park shuttle are permitted. Development has been limited to construction of a handsome new pier which extends 1,225 feet out on San Pablo Bay.

The concrete pier was completed in 1977 near the site of the Hercules Wharf where vessels docked to load explosives. When the super-structure of the old wharf was dismantled, the pilings were left intact. This was because pilings provide homes for a variety of marine life on which perch and other fish feed. Mainstays of the catch at Point Pinole are flounder, perch, jacksmelt, kingfish, and sharks. A few striped bass are caught and, on rare occasions, someone is lucky enough to hook a salmon.

There's no entry fee at Point Pinole, but the park charges $1.00 for parking. From the parking lot just inside the entrance gate, it's a hike of 1½ miles to the fishing pier. For 25 cents, anglers may ride to the pier on the park shuttle which operates from 8:30 A.M. to 6:00 P.M. daily. Fishing parties are advised to bring their own bait and lunches as there is no place in or near the park where these may be purchased.

LOCATION:
On the south shore of San Pablo Bay due west of Pinole.

HOW TO GET THERE:
*Auto:* From Interstate 80, drive west on Hilltop Drive to San Pablo Avenue. Turn right on San Pablo and then left on Atlas Road. Park entrance is near the intersection of Atlas and the Giant Highway.
*Public Transportation:* AC Transit Bus No. 78 runs to Point Pinole Monday through Saturday. Connects with BART at the Richmond Station.

FACILITIES:
Benches with windscreens on the pier. Drinking fountain and rest rooms at the foot of the pier. Shaded picnic sites with benches and tables. Beach path, horse and bicycle trails.

HOURS:
8:00 A.M. to 5:00 P.M.—Winter.
8:00 A.M. to 10:00 P.M.—When Daylight Saving Time is in Effect.

Pedestrians may enter the park any time except during curfew hours—10:00 P.M. to 5:00 A.M.

ADMINISTRATION:
East Bay Regional Park District, 11500 Skyline Boulevard, Oakland 94619 (415) 531-9300.

An open-air surrey shuttles fishermen back and forth between the pier at Point Pinole and the nearest A.C. Transit bus stop.

# 23. Rodeo

Rodeo on the south shore of San Pablo Bay was the site of rodeos and, no doubt, some colorful fiestas under Mexican rule. A century later, it gained notoriety as one of the small towns on old US 40 where Sunday traffic was often reduced to a crawl. The congestion ended with the completion of Interstate 80.

Presently, Rodeo attracts few outsiders other than fishermen who find the Bay here especially abundant in striped bass and sturgeon. Pier fishing is provided by Frank Joseph's Resort on Lone Tree Point. This rustic establishment antedates most other fishing piers in the Bay Area. The catch includes perch, jacksmelt, flounder, skates, and sharks. The fee for use of the pier is fifty cents.

LOCATION:
Next door to Rodeo Marina at the foot of Pacific Avenue.

HOW TO GET THERE:
*Auto:* Leave Interstate 80 for Rodeo at Willow Avenue exit. Follow Willow to Parker. Proceed north on Parker and Pacific streets to the waterfront.
*Public Transportation:* AC Transit Bus No. 78A to Crockett stops at Rodeo. This bus operates only on weekdays.

FACILITIES:
Benches with windbreaks on the pier. Restaurant, snack bar, bait sales, and rest rooms.

HOURS:
6:30 A.M. to 6:00 P.M., daily.

ADMINISTRATION:
Joseph's Fishing Resort (415) 799-4452.

A proud fisherman displays a modest-sized white sturgeon and two very respectable stripers caught along the Contra Costa shore.

# 24. Crockett

Crockett at the west end of the Carquinez Strait was a busy port when paddlewheel steamers plied the Bay. It is now an antiquated village with a population of 3,500. Its only industry is the waterfront refinery of the California and Hawaiian Sugar company which has been in business there since 1906. For better than thirty years, anglers have patronized the private fishing pier situated west of the refinery off Dowrelio Road.

This weathered pier extends from frontage occupied by a seafood restaurant and the Crockett Marine Service, which manages the pier and operates a fleet of sport fishing charter boats. The pier fee is fifty cents. Some big sturgeon have been taken here but, as elsewhere on the upper bay, the most sought-after fish are flounder and striped bass. In early season, youngsters catch quite a few "piling perch," a local name for redtail surfperch.

LOCATION:
Foot of Port Street off Dowrelio Road, Crockett.

HOW TO GET THERE:
*Auto:* From Interstate 80, take Crockett exit to Pomona Street, turn left on Port Street, and left again at the foot of Port on Dowrelio Road.

*Public Transportation:* AC Transit Bus No. 78A runs to Crockett on weekdays only.

FACILITIES:
Snack bar with bait sales and rest rooms. The Nantucket Fish Company features seafood dinners prepared Eastern style.

HOURS:
Closes in summer at 7:30 P.M.

ADMINISTRATION:
Crockett Marine Service, Foot of Port Street, Crockett (415) 787-1047.

Interstate 80 vaults Carquinez Strait just beyond fishermen at Crockett's fishing pier, a hot spot for stripers in the fall.

# 25. Vallejo

Perhaps the largest fish ever taken from a Bay Area pier was caught January 11, 1980, in the brackish estuary of the Napa River at Vallejo Public Pier. Bottom fishing with 25 pound test line and a live six-inch gobie mudsucker, George Gano of Vallejo hooked a white sturgeon which weighed 194 pounds and measured eight feet in length. The battle that ensued lasted two hours and 45 minutes.

There was no way a fish this size could be hoisted to the pier. Fortunately for George Gano, two boat fishermen were on hand to gaff the exhausted sturgeon and haul it ashore.

One of the first things a visitor is apt to remark about the Vallejo Pier is the bumpy surface of the platform. The pier got this way through years of service as part of a drawbridge which linked the mainland with Mare Island. After its replacement by a high-rise structure, about a thousand feet of the old span were reconstructed as a fishing pier. Shortly after the pier opened to the public in 1971, it became popular as one of the few good shore fishing spots in the Bay Area to try for the elusive white sturgeon.

On a good day at the pier, as many as a dozen sturgeon are hooked and perhaps two or three legal-sized fish are successfuly landed. However, a preponderance of the annual catch are throwbacks which fall short of the 40-inch minimum length.

Fish caught at the pier in far greater numbers than sturgeon include jacksmelt, starry flounder, and striped bass. Many of the stripers hooked during summer are less than legal size. To reduce injuries to undersized bass, the Fish and Game Department recommends use of hooks at least half an inch wide between the point and the shank.

HOW TO GET THERE:
*Auto:* From Interstate 80 or US 101 by way of California Highway 37 (Sears Point Road) to Wilson Avenue at the east end of the Napa River Bridge.
*Public Transportation:* Vallejo Transit Lines Bus No. 1 (California Meadow Springs to Wilson Avenue).

FACILITIES:
Benches, lights, fish cleaning sink, rest rooms, bait sales, and snack shop.

HOURS:
Pier open 24 hours, daily.

Greater Vallejo Recreation District, 395 Amador, Vallejo (707) 642-7556.

NOTES:
The prevailing wind often complicates fishing at Vallejo Pier. It causes lines to billow, making it difficult for the angler to detect a bite. Sinkers may drift, with the result that two or more lines cross and become hopelessly entangled. A solution to both problems, when the tide is right, is to cast with the wind to a spot remote from where other fishermen have dropped their lines. But when the tide is moving counter to the wind, the old hands at Vallejo Pier turn to balloon fishing.

A toy balloon is blown up and closed with a knot. The tag end of the knot is threaded on a wire snap where the leader is joined to the main line. The rig is then gently lowered to the water and permitted to drift with the tide. When it reaches the desired distance from the pier, the fisherman heaves back on the line so the balloon tears free and the sinker takes the bait to the bottom.

The pier provides an interesting view of the Mare Island Naval Shipyard. Other than naval vessels, river traffic consists mainly of fuel barges and small pleasure craft.

# 26. Martinez

The long, trim public fishing pier at Martinez was reconstructed in the early 1970's from a landing used by the Bay Area's last automobile ferry. Resting now in a slip next to the pier is the steel-hulled, 251-foot-long *Fresno*, a steam-powered ferry built in 1927. It made its final 15-minute trip of the line across Suisun Bay the day before the Benicia-Martinez Bridge opened in 1961.

The fishing pier is part of a 200-acre waterfront recreation complex which adjoins the tanker docks of the Shell Oil Company. Martinez dates back to Gold Rush days. It's so rich in history that guidebooks tend to overlook an event here of great significance to Bay Area anglers. It was at Martinez in 1879 that a rail shipment of 132 live baby striped bass was delivered to the bay. A second plant of 300 stripers was made near Martinez in 1882. These 432 fish were the ancestors of all striped bass present in West Coast waters today.

Aside from stripers, large numbers of starry flounder and an occasional big sturgeon are caught at Martinez Pier. Flounder fishing is apt to be most productive from December through early spring.

The old ferry slip has been converted into a new fishing pier.

LOCATION:
Foot of North Court Street, Martinez.

HOW TO GET THERE:
*Auto:* Leave Interstate 80 on Martinez exit and drive west on Marina Vista to Court Street.
*Public Transportation:* Go Greyhound or take the BART express bus that leaves for Martinez from the BART station at Concord.

FACILITIES:
Benches, fish cleaning sink, rest rooms (at Marina headquarters), bait shop, and restaurant. Close by is a nice park with benches, tables, and grills.

HOURS:
7:00 A.M. to dusk, daily.

ADMINISTRATION:
City of Martinez Recreation Department, 525 Henrietta, Martinez (415) 372-4940.

NOTES:
Martinez Regional Shoreline is under development near the pier. This is a cooperative project of the City of Martinez, State Lands Commission, Shell Oil Company, and East Bay Regional Park District to provide a shoreline park with two miles of trails.

# 27. Benicia

Benicia, which once housed the state capitol, doesn't have a public pier reserved for sport fishing. Now in the throes of industrial and residential expansion, this historic port on the Carquinez Strait has big plans for its waterfront. It may get a fishing pier when a 300-berth marina (still on the drawing board) is completed at the foot of First Street. Meanwhile, anglers may try their luck at the minipier which adjoins a public boat ramp at the foot of Ninth Street.

Young people catch mostly small bullheads here during summer. The best action occurs in autumn and early spring when striped bass are hooked off the pier on plugs and other artificials as well as bait. Flounder fishing usually holds up from late winter through spring.

LOCATION:
Foot of Ninth Street, Benicia.

HOW TO GET THERE:
*Auto:* Interstate 680.
*Public Transportation:* Benica-Vallejo Stage Line operates bus service between Vallejo and Benicia. Buses leave every two hours, Monday through Saturday.

FACILITIES:
Drinking fountain and rest rooms. Launching facility adjoins park with public beach and a picnic area with benches, tables, and grills.

HOURS:
Pier open during daylight hours, daily.

ADMINISTRATION:
City of Benicia, 250 East "L", Benicia (707) 745-0510.

NOTES:
Sturgeon to 140 pounds were reported caught at and near the Ninth Street Pier in March and April of 1980.

A Dodger fan hoists a stringer of bullheads, a summer catch on Benicia's Ninth Street Pier. Stripers bite here in the fall.

# 28. East Fort Baker

Fort Baker, established in 1897, is the oldest of three forts on the Marin Headlands which once guarded the Golden Gate with big guns and later with Nike missiles.

Forts Barry and Cronkite and a portion of Fort Baker are now administered by the Park Service as part of the Golden Gate National Recreation Area. All of Fort Baker lies within the boundaries of the GGNRA but 650 acres which extend east of the Golden Gate Bridge remain under the jurisdiction of the Army. Here an old military wharf on Horseshoe Bay has served as a public fishing pier for many years.

A variety of perch are caught at the pier, which sometimes provides excellent angling for both jacksmelt and top smelt. The pier is not recommended for small children because it lacks guard rails. Fishing is permitted at Point Cavallo and from the breakwater that shelters a small boat harbor in Horseshoe Bay.

LOCATION:
Off Alexander Avenue west of Sausalito and east of the Golden Gate Bridge.

HOW TO GET THERE:
*Auto:* Leave US 101 at the Alexander Avenue exit, which is the first exit beyond the GGNRA Vista Point. Shortly after leaving the freeway turn left on Danes Drive and then, just before the tunnel, turn right onto Bunker Road.
*Public Transportation:* None.

FACILITIES:
Rest rooms.

HOURS:
Gates on roads entering and leaving the reservation open at 7:00 A.M. and close at 5:00 P.M.

ADMINISTRATION:
United States Army. For general information on the Marin Headlands unit of the Golden Gate National Recreation Area, call (415) 561-7612.

NOTES:
It is anticipated that eventually East Fort Baker will become part of the Golden Gate National Recreation Area. Proposals for development include establishment of picnic grounds, wading beach, restaurant or snack shop, youth hostel, and a ferry landing.

There is good fishing off both the pier and jetty.

NORTH BAY PIERS

# 29. Sausalito

Sausalito owes much of its charm as a fishing spot to geography and some timely legislation. Steep hillsides confine the business district to a narrow, wave-lapped ledge on Richardson Bay. Here, Bridgeway Boulevard, the town's only main street, is lined with restaurants, boutiques, and numerous arts and crafts shops interspersed with wharves, marinas, mini-parks, and a long stretch of unobstructed seawall.

A number of private wharves, as well as the municipal seawall, are open to fishing thanks to enactment of the McAteer-Petris Act in 1965. Among other things, the act requires that public access to the waterfront be provided to the maximum extent possible in new developments on San Francisco Bay.

One of the favorite fishing spots on the Bridgeway is the pier where the Ondine and Trident Restaurants are situated. Smelt fishing is often good here and on the adjoing seawall where a sidewalk parallel to the main promenade has been installed for anglers and boat watchers.

Sausalito's waterfront is one of the few places on the Bay where Pacific herring are caught from shore. Huge schools of herring enter the Golden Gate from December through March to deposit their eggs on rocks and dock pilings.

Spawning mainly occurs around islands and inaccessible cliff areas. But usually, for a week or so, the fish swarm off the seawall during the highest stage of the tide.

Within minutes after the local grapevine signals the arrival of a herring run, the docks and seawall become lined elbow-to-elbow with people furiously working dip nets. After the tide begins to ebb and the herring become less numerous, anglers catch them with artificial flies. When hooked on light tackle, a foot-long herring is apt to display the same sporting quality as a freshwater trout of commensurate size.

Poke poling is another kind of fishing popular on the Sausalito waterfront. Tackle consists of a cane or fiberglass pole to which is wired a six-inch length of hook and line baited with a slice of anchovy. The bait is poked into crevices of the sea wall and other rocky places along the waterfront where rock eels and cabezone dwell.

LOCATION:
In Marin County on the west shore of Richardson Bay.

HOW TO GET THERE:
*Auto:* Leave US 101 at the Alexander Avenue

exit, turn right on Second Street and then right on Richardson Street.

*Public Transportation:* From San Francisco, take Golden Gate Transit Bus No. 10 or the Golden Gate Transit ferry which runs from the Ferry Building to Sausalito. For information, call (415) 332-6600.

FACILITIES:
Public rest rooms located on bay side of Bridgeway Boulevard near intersection with Bay Street. Choice of city parks for a picnic. Restaurants abound, but most are expensive.

HOURS:
Pier open 24 hours, daily.

ADMINISTRATION:
Waterfront parks administered by the Sausalito Recreation Department, 420 Litho, Sausalito, California (415) 332-4520.

NOTES:
The name Sausalito derives from a Spanish word meaning "little grove of willows." In 1775, Richardson Bay provided an anchorage for the first Spanish ship known to navigate the Golden Gate. A British sailor, William A. Richardson, obtained a grant to *Rancho Saucelito* in 1838. In the early days of settle-

ment when Sausalito was patronized by the crews of whaling ships and men-o-war, it gained a reputation comparable to that of San Francisco's Barbary Coast. But, for most of its existence, the town was a quiet fishing port where Marin commuters took the ferry to San Francisco.

After a brief flurry of shipbuilding in World War II, Sausalito became the residence of many writers, artists, and colorful personalities. Most fled to the North Coast with Sausalito's rise to prominence as a tourist attraction and recreation spot for weekenders.

# 30. Elephant Rock

Elephant Rock Pier, located on the tip of the hilly Tiburon Peninsula, is a captivating mini-pier reserved for fishing by boys and girls under sixteen years of age. This innovative wooden structure encircles and is partially supported by a pyramid-shaped rock that rises a few yards offshore on Raccoon Strait. Perch and smelt fishing is often good here.

The rocky shore which extends west of the pier to the Tiburon ferry landing is popular with shore fishermen. Good lure casting for striped bass has been reported here in autumn, when schools of these fish pass through Raccoon Strait on their annual migration to the upper bay and Delta area.

Directly across Raccoon Strait from the pier looms Angel Island. Formerly a military reservation, the island's 740 acres of woods and grasslands are now managed as a state park. Hiking trails here lead to a number of places along the shore which invite fishing for perch and rockfish. The island may be approached on ferries that operate from Tiburon, Berkeley, and San Francisco.

LOCATION:
Point Tiburon on the Tiburon Peninsula in Marin County.

HOW TO GET THERE:
*Auto:* Leave US 101 at Tiburon exit and proceed west on State Highway 131 to the intersection of Paradise Drive with Mar West Street.
*Public Transportation:* From San Francisco, take Golden Gate Transit Bus No. 10 or the Harbor Carriers ferry.

The Harbor Carriers operate a commuter ferry from San Francisco to Tiburon on weekdays. Another ferry of the Red and White Fleet makes daily runs between San Francisco, Angel Island, and Tiburon in summer and on weekends and holidays in winter. These ferries may dock in San Francisco at the Ferry Building or at Fisherman's Wharf. For information, call (415) 398-1141.

The Harbor Carriers also operate a ferry between Berkeley and Angel Island on weekends from April through October. For information, call (415) 398-1141. Another operator runs a ferry between Tiburon and Angel Island. This boat operates daily from June through Labor Day and on weekends and holidays in winter. For information, call (415) 435-2131.

**FACILITIES:**
Restaurant adjoins the pier. It is a short walk
west on Paradise Drive to the ferry landing and
more restaurants in the village of Tiburon which
has some interesting shops.

**HOURS:**
No hours posted.

**ADMINISTRATION:**
Tiburon Parks and Recreation, 101 Esperanza,
Tiburon (415) 435-4355.

# 31. Paradise Beach

The lovely site of Paradise Beach County Park is one of the oldest waterfront recreation spots on the Bay. Long before it became accessible by road and a park was developed, affluent weekenders sailed here in their yachts to camp, fish, and laze on the beach.

The park has lots of green lawn, attractive picnic facilities, and a recently renovated fishing pier which commands a sweeping view of the upper bay. Perch, smelt, and flounder predominate in the catch at this pier.

The most important attribute of Paradise Beach in terms of fishing is its sheltered location on the lee side of the Tiburon Peninsula. The prevailing wind, which so often is the bane of anglers elsewhere on the Bay, rarely presents a problem here.

LOCATION:
On the east shore of the Tiburon Peninsula ten miles south of San Rafael.

HOW TO GET THERE:
*Auto:* Leave US 101 at Tiburon exit and drive west on State Highway 131. Turn left on Trestle Glen Boulevard and then right on Paradise Drive.
*Public Transportation:* None.

FACILITIES:
$1.00 charge for parking. Pier has benches, tap water, and fish sinks. Rest rooms, picnic benches and tables with charcoal grills, and small wading beach are nearby.

HOURS:
Park open from 10:00 A.M. to 7:00 P.M., daily.

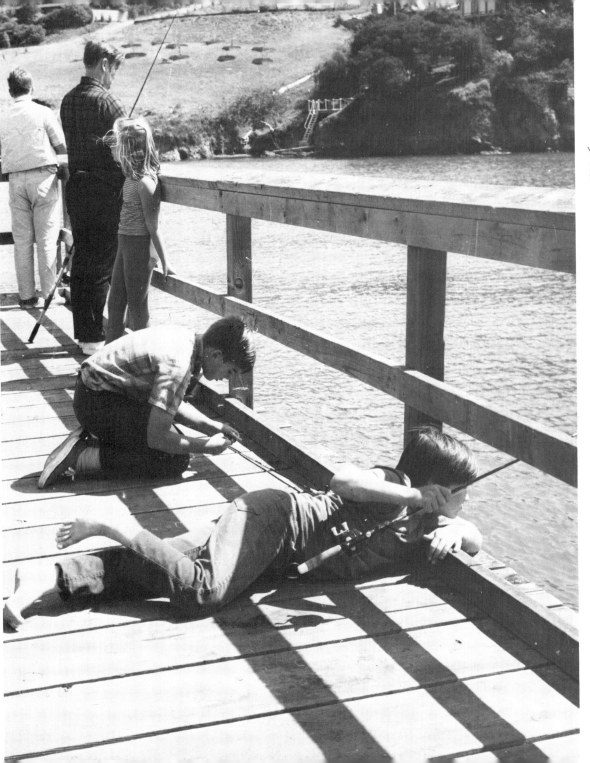

Youngsters wait for
perch or flounder
to bite.

# 32. Pacifica

Pacifica Pier is unique for two reasons. It alone of Bay Area piers juts into the angry surf which pounds the seashore outside the Golden Gate. It's the only public pier on the outer coast from California to Alaska where persistent fishermen stand a reasonable chance of hooking both striped bass and Pacific salmon.

This prestressed concrete structure was built expressly for sport fishing in the early 1970's at a cost of $2 million. From Sharp Park beach, it runs a thousand feet out to sea and then makes a 90 degree turn to provide more fishing access where the water is 32 feet deep. The pier's high platform, clean lines, and long spans between pilings were designed to reduce the impact of the crashing breakers.

Typically on a summer day at Pacifica, the coastal fog clears just long enough to accommodate a leisurely lunch break. But a paucity of sunshine in no way diminishes the pier's popularity.

On weekends from late spring through early autumn, it's usual to find both sides of the pier lined with people fishing elbow-to-elbow. Heedless of wind, fog, or drizzle, whole families come prepared to spend the entire day. It's a fair walk out on the pier from the parking area.

So backpacks and shopping carts are creatively employed to bring folding chairs, picnic baskets, thermos jugs, ice boxes, radios, paperbacks, and backgammon sets together with bait buckets, ring nets, rod holders, and tackle boxes.

In the first part of July in 1980, up to seventy salmon a day were reported taken at Pacifica Pier on anchovies. The fish ranged from ten to thirty pounds in weight. Normally on a good day, about a dozen salmon are hooked, of which five or six are successfully hoisted to the pier. It's a trick to land a salmon, striped bass, or fish of any size at Pacifica because the platform is situated so high above the water. The fisherman requires the help of another person to secure his catch by means of a rope attached to a ring net or weighted gaff.

Next to salmon, the fish most prized at Pacifica are halibut and striped bass. The action can be fast and furious when a school of hungry stripers follows a bait school inshore to the vicinity of the pier. A preponderance of the daily catch consists of perch, flounder, sand dabs, jacksmelt, kingfish (white croaker), tomcods, sculpins, and skates. Impressive numbers of crabs are taken with ring nets.

From late December through January, people come to the pier to watch and photograph the grey whales that pass by on their annual migration from the Arctic to Baja California.

LOCATION:
Foot of Santa Rosa Avenue off Beach Boulevard in the Sharp Park district of Pacifica.

HOW TO GET THERE:
*Auto:* Highway 1 to Paloma Avenue exit. At west end of Paloma, turn left on Beach Boulevard.
*Public Transportation:* From Daly City BART, take SamTrans Bus No. 1-A to Pacifica.

FACILITIES:
Drinking fountain, benches, lighting, rest rooms, and fish cleaning facility. Snack shop with bait and tackle sales.

HOURS:
Pier Closing Hours: Winter Season 8:00 P.M.
                    Spring Season 9:00 P.M.
                    Summer Season 10:00 P.M.
                    Fall Season 9:00 P.M.

ADMINISTRATION:
Pacifica Parks, Beaches and Recreation, 170 Santa Maria Avenue, Pacifica (415) 877-8631.

A persistent fisherman shows off his catch of salmon.

NOTES:
Pier patrolled by park rangers. No inboard or overhead casts permitted.

# 33. Half Moon Bay

On Half Moon Bay off Coast Highway 1 at El Granada, two rock jetties, each about 1½ miles long, enclose Pillar Point Harbor. The main function of the county wharf here is to provide a landing for sports and commercial fishing boats. However, extensions of the pier near shore often afford good perch fishing. Angling is permitted off both of the rock jetties. The catch off the East Jetty consists mainly of perch, flounder, and kingfish. Cabezon, striped seaperch, greenling seatrout, and other fish which favor rocky areas comprise most of the catch off the west jetty. Striped bass may occasionally be hooked off either jetty.

When jetty fishing, old hands use a tobacco sack filled with sand in place of a lead sinker. This is because lead sinkers are too easily snagged on the rocks. A state fishing license is required to fish from the jetties and anywhere along shore except on the public pier.

LOCATION:
San Mateo Coast at El Granada.

HOW TO GET THERE:
*Auto:* From State Highway 1, turn west on Capistrano Road.
*Public Transportation:* SamTrans Bus No. 90H stops near the pier. This bus operates daily except Sunday from downtown San Mateo to points on the coast from the town of Half Moon Bay north to Montara.

FACILITIES:
Drinking fountain, rest rooms, restaurant, snack shop, and bait store where tackle may be rented.

HOURS:
Pier open 24 hours, daily.

ADMINISTRATION:
San Mateo County Harbor District, Pillar Point Harbormaster (415) 726-5727. Pillar Point Harbor Patrol (415) 726-4382.

Commercial fisherman unloads catch at county pier on Half Moon Bay.

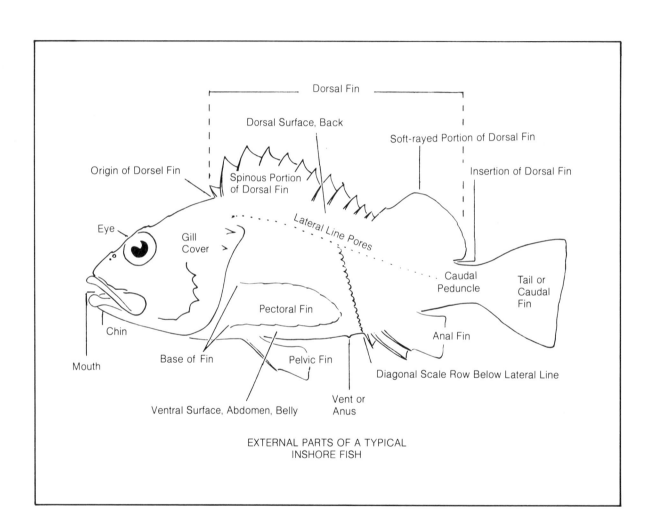

EXTERNAL PARTS OF A TYPICAL
INSHORE FISH

# IV
# Fish Most Commonly Caught At Piers

## CROAKERS

Croakers are commonly known as drums on the East Coast. Both names derive from the odd sound male croakers make through rapid contractions of their swimbladders. The croaker family, *Sciaenidae*, is represented by nine species in California waters, of which the white seabass is most prized by anglers.

Croakers, which contribute heavily to the sport catch in Southern California, include black, white, and yellowfin croakers, the little queenfish, and the highly esteemed California corbina. In the Bay Area, only the white croaker

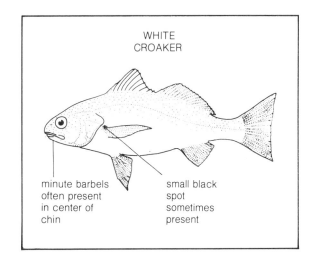

WHITE CROAKER

minute barbels often present in center of chin

small black spot sometimes present

or kingfish is caught in significant numbers by anglers.

### IDENTIFICATION
All croakers have two dorsal fins. The first dorsal fin is roughly triangular in shape. The pelvic fin has one spine and five soft rays. Most species have barbels under the chin.

### KINGFISH OR WHITE CROAKER
Kingfish is the popular name for white croakers in the Bay Area. These silvery fish rarely exceed a pound in weight or a foot in length. When kingfish school off a pier, they are apt to take any fresh bait and not infrequently hook themselves in the process. Some fishermen deplore this species for a lack of sporting quality. However, kingfish are important to the pier fishery in that they often provide good action when other fish are scarce or not biting.

Kingfish are easy to tell apart from other croakers because they have from twelve to fiteen spines in the first dorsal fin. No other croaker has more than eleven spines in this fin.

### WHITE SEABASS
Years ago, white seabass were fairly abundant in the San Francisco area. They are uncommon now, possibly because of a shift in ocean currents or the scarcity of Pacific sardines. In recent years there have been a few reports of white seabass caught from the public pier at Pacifica.

### COOKING SUGGESTIONS
Some anglers consider kingfish a delicacy and many pounds of this species are sold in fish markets. Yet the notion persists that kingfish make poor tablefare. This may be because, when kingfish are undercooked, the flesh is rendered overly soft and tasteless. For good eating, anglers partial to the kingfish say it should be fried to a crisp.

## FLATFISH

The order of flatfish, *Heterosomata*, is divided into several families. All flatfish caught in the Bay belong to either the left-eyed flounder family, *Bothidae*, or the right-eyed flounder family, *Pleuronectidae*.

For a brief period after it hatches, a baby flatfish has an eye on either side of the head the same as a perch. But soon one eye migrates to a position close to the other eye. The eyed side of an adult flatfish is heavily pigmented. The blind side is usually white.

Flatfish form an important part of the commercial catch in California waters. The leading commercial species include English sole, Dover sole, rex sole, and California halibut. Of these, the halibut is most prized by anglers but, in terms of numbers caught, the starry flounder is the most important flatfish in the Bay.

### STARRY FLOUNDER

The starry flounder may be easily identified by its orange-tinted fins that are striped with black bars. The fish is named for its tiny star-shaped scales. It feeds mainly on clams, crabs, and various crustaceans. Large specimens may feed on small fish, such as anchovy and shiner perch. Starry flounders have been reported in weights to twenty pounds. Those caught off piers average about two pounds. The eyed side of this species is pigmented in shadings that may change to match the color of the ocean bottom where the fish happens to be.

Ichthyologists classify the starry flounder as *euryhaline*, which means it ordinarily lives in saltwater but sometimes moves into freshwater. In the Northwest starry flounder have been caught 75 miles up the Columbia River. The fish may frequent mud, sand, or gravel bottoms but never rocky areas. Although not a leading commercial species, starry flounder often appear in fish markets as fillet of sole.

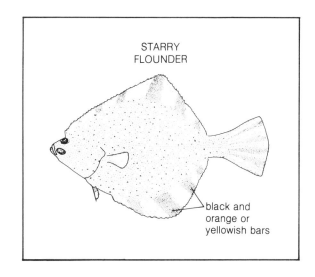

STARRY FLOUNDER

black and orange or yellowish bars

As game fish, starry flounder are not noted for savage strikes or fancy acrobatics. An angler may not know when a flounder takes the bait unless the rod is hand held or a small bell is hung on the rod tip. Once hooked, a flounder resists being reeled in by swimming backwards or by trying to bury itself on the bottom. It stands a good chance of dislodging the hook should the angler attempt to "horse in" the fish.

A standard saltwater leader is used for flounder with a pyramid sinker clipped to the end or with a sliding sinker threaded on the main line.

Hooks as small as Nos. 4 or 6 are preferred because the starry flounder has a small mouth. Ghost shrimp, clams, mussels, and most any cutbait may attract flounder. Sometimes, these fish will ignore a stationary bait. They may be more inclined to bite when the bait is retrieved slowly across the bottom.

Starry flounder may be caught any time of year in the Bay. The prime months are from December through April when these fish move inshore to spawn. At this time, all the piers listed in the North Bay section of this book are recommended. Other likely hotspots include the piers at Fort Baker, Emeryville, and Candlestick Point Park.

CALIFORNIA HALIBUT
The California halibut is a splendid game fish caught in very limited numbers by pier fishermen. Most taken from piers are hooked by anglers fishing primarily for striped bass with a live mudsucker or shiner perch as bait. A twelve-pound halibut is considered trophy size on the piers, but this species has been reported by commercial fishermen to sixty pounds in weight and as long as five feet.

When a California halibut is hooked, it makes a ferocious bid for freedom with long powerful runs. The challenge for the angler is to keep the fish from placing undue strain on the line while avoiding any slack. Given the least bit of slack, the fish may throw the hook. But if the pressure on the line is too great, the hook will tear free from the halibut's delicate mouth tissues. A net or gaff should be used to lift the fish to the pier.

SANDDABS
Sanddabs make excellent tablefish, as demonstrated by the fact that many seafood restaurants in the Bay Area feature them as a delicacy. Adult sanddabs average about eight inches in length but may grow to a foot or more. Both speckled and Pacific sanddabs are taken in limited numbers at piers on the lower bay and at Pacifica on the San Mateo Coast. Boat fishermen account for most of the sport catch because sanddabs favor fairly deep water.

COOKING SUGGESTIONS
When properly dressed, a flounder or halibut should yield four boneless fillets, two from each side. The quick way to a delicious meal is to sprinkle the fillets with salt and pepper, dust with flour, fry on both sides to a golden brown, and serve with lemon wedges or tartar sauce.

Sanddabs are rarely filleted because of their small size. There are some fancy ways to prepare sanddabs but Eddie Viarengo, who tends the fish counter at Trag's Market in San Mateo, recommends pan frying. He says to trim the fins after the sanddabs have been gutted, scaled, and beheaded. Then rinse the fish, pat with paper towels, roll in seasoned flour, and quick fry in enough oil to cover the pan. Viarengo cautions that the oil must be brought to a medium-high heat before the sanddabs are placed in the pan. Otherwise, the fish will stick to the pan and fall apart when the cook tries to remove them to a plate.

Flounder and halibut fillets make excellent fish and chips. A book of favorite recipes compiled by the Junior Matrons of the San Mateo Buddhist Temple features this recipe:

### FISH 'N CHIPS
| | |
|---|---|
| 2 | pounds fresh fish |
| 1 | cup flour |
| 1 | teaspoon salt |
| ½ | to ¾ teaspoon baking powder |
| 1⅛ | cup of water |
| 2 | tablespoons of oil |
| | Bread crumbs |

Mix flour, salt and baking powder. Add water and stir to consistency of runny pancake batter. Fold in oil.

Dip fish in batter and roll in bread crumbs. Lay on paper towels and refrigerate overnight or at least three hours. Deep fry in oil, barely covering fish. Drain. (Turns a lovely brown and should be eaten soon after cooking.) Serve with a tartar sauce.

Can be served with chips (French fried potatoes) or rice.

Yo Inouye

## SHARKS AND RAYS

Sharks and rays differ from most other kinds of fish by having skeletons composed of cartilage instead of bone. In place of scales, they have thin hides covered with minute protrusions that are very hard. The skin of some sharks is so tough and abrasive that it is used in some industrial processes as sandpaper.

There are more than 250 species of sharks in the world. Six are common in San Francisco Bay. The species most frequently caught from piers are the leopard shark and the brown smoothhound shark. Both fish are members of

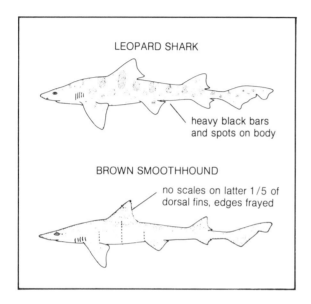

LEOPARD SHARK

heavy black bars
and spots on body

BROWN SMOOTHHOUND

no scales on latter 1/5 of
dorsal fins, edges frayed

leopard sharks are good eating, many, if not most, pier fishermen regard them as trash fish. Quite a few that are caught off the piers are left behind for the gulls.

Sharks are especially numerous in the South Bay where they not only prey on small fish but act as scavengers. A marine biologist once remarked that without sharks San Francisco Bay would be too polluted for people to live near its shores.

The order of rays, *Batoidei*, is represented in California by the bat ray, three species of stingrays, and six species of skates. Stingrays are common in bays and off beaches along the Southern California coast. The fish Bay Area anglers usually refer to as a stingray, or "stingaree," is the bat ray which is the lone representative in California waters of the eagle ray family, *Myliobatidae*.

The bat ray has teeth capable of crushing oysters. This formidable predator of mollusks and crustaceans grows to four feet in width. It has been known to attain weights in excess of 200 pounds. The stinger is a sharp spine located in front of the whip-like tail just behind the dorsal fin. The stings are venomous and capable of inflicting very painful lesions. For first

the smoothhound family, *Triakidae*. They look alike except for their coloration. The brown smoothhound is bronze or brownish whereas the leopard shark is grayish with black spots and crossbars.

The popular name for the brown smoothhound shark in the Bay Area is sand shark. It grows to three feet in length. Leopard sharks have been reported to six feet but most taken by anglers measure less than three feet. Although sand and

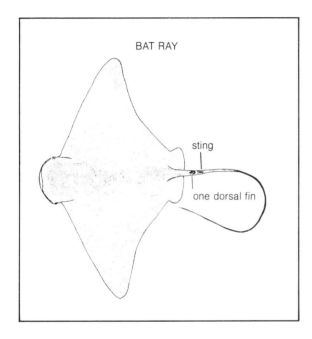

BAT RAY

sting

one dorsal fin

ior to that of any fish in the Bay. It is difficult to know to what extent bat rays are hooked from piers, especially because anglers often mistake skates for stingrays.

Skates of the family *Rajidae* are more or less diamond-shaped with "wings" (pectoral fins) the same as a bat ray. However, instead of a stinger, there are a number of small spines along the tail which are not poisonous. Skates have two dorsal fins, the bat ray has one, and stingrays have none.

The skates most commonly caught in San Francisco Bay are the big skate and California skate. The latter fish occurs in shades of dark olive to brown. It rarely grows longer than two feet or so whereas the big skate which may be colored brown or dark gray has been reported in lengths to eight feet.

### ANGLING

Some of the regulars throw up their hands in disgust and go home when sharks happen to be the only fish biting off a pier. The prejudice against sharks runs deep. However, complaints these fish lack sporting quality are usually heard from an individual who just landed a baby shark with tackle heavy enought to subdue a big sturgeon. A good place to sample

aid, a Fish and Game Department publication recommends cleaning the wound and soaking it in water as hot as the injured person can stand. Early on, a doctor should be seen to control possible secondary infection.

A San Francisco partyboat skipper who used to catch bat rays for exhibit at an amusement park claimed their sporting quality was super-

shark fishing is the San Mateo pier on the South Bay. Sharks are so abundant in this part of the Bay that anglers often refer to it as "shark heaven."

A strip of anchovy or Pacific sardine is good bait for sharks. Skates are partial to mussel or clam bait. Most sharks and skates hooked off piers run to a size that can be handled with the lightest tackle recommended for striped bass. A large skate, however, can be very tough to budge, should it cup its "wings" to form a vacuum on the bottom.

COOKING SUGGESTIONS
The folklore is widespread that sharks and skates are not good to eat. Among old hands on the piers, there seems to be a consensus that both sharks and skates are edible but not palatable. So it's small wonder these species rarely turn up in fish markets.

According to a team of experts on seafood and nutrition at the University of California, "Properly prepared for the table, shark and skate taste very much like other popular food fishes. Cooked shark meat is firm and rather suggests that of swordfish in texture. Skate has a delicate texture and flavor. Both shark and skate are high in protein, low in fat, and are usually more economical than the better known species of fish."

Raymond D. Cannon in his book, *How To Fish The Pacific Coast*, relates that, during World War II, many thousands of pounds of shark meat were colored and sold as salmon as well as fillet of sole, halibut, and swordfish. Apparently, there were few complaints.

Both sharks and skates may be baked, broiled, poached, or pan fried, using most any recipe that is recommended for lean fish. Here are some suggestions from the Marine Advisory Programs at University of California, Davis.

OVEN FRIED SHARK OR SKATE
2 lbs shark fillets or skate wings
½ cup milk
1½ tablespoons salt
1 cup fine bread crumbs
⅓ cup cooking oil

Wipe fillets or chunks of skate wings with a damp cloth and dry thoroughly. Add salt to milk, stir until dissolved. Dip each fillet first in milk, then in bread crumbs, and lay on a greased shallow baking pan. Top each layer of fish with the cooking oil, and bake in a preheated oven at 375°F for 25 minutes.

## ORIENTAL SHARK STEAKS

2 lbs shark steaks or other fish steaks, fresh or frozen
¼ cup orange juice
¼ cup soy sauce
2 tablespoons catsup
2 tablespoons melted fat or oil
2 tablespoons chopped parsley
1 tablespoon lemon juice
1 clove garlic, finely chopped
½ teaspoon oregano
½ teaspoon pepper

Thaw frozen steaks. Cut into serving-size portions and place in a single layer in a shallow baking dish. Combine remaining ingredients. Pour sauce over fish and let stand for 30 minutes, turning once. Remove fish, reserving sauce for basting. Place fish in well-greased, hinged wire grills. Cook about 4 inches from moderately hot coals for 8 minutes. Baste with sauce. Turn and cook 7 to 10 minutes longer or until fish flakes easily when tested with a fork. Serves six.

## BARBECUED SHARK STEAKS

2 pounds shark steaks or other fish steaks, fresh or frozen
¼ cup chopped onion
2 tablespoons chopped green pepper
1 clove garlic, finely chopped
2 tablespoons melted fat or oil
1 can (8 ounces) tomato sauce
2 tablespoons lemon juice
1 tablespoon Worcestershire sauce
1 tablespoon sugar
2 teaspoons salt
¼ teaspoon pepper

Thaw frozen steaks. Cook onion, green pepper, and garlic in fat until tender. Add remaining ingredients and simmer for 5 minutes, stirring occasionally. Cool. Cut steaks into serving-size portions and place in a single layer in a shallow baking dish. Pour sauce over fish and let stand for 30 minutes, turning once. Remove fish, reserving sauce for basting. Place fish in well-greased, hinged wire grills. Cook about 4 inches from moderately hot coals for 8 minutes. Baste with sauce. Turn and cook for 7 to 10 minutes longer or until fish flakes easily when tested with a fork. Serves six.

## SKATE KABOBS

2 pounds skate wings or other fish fillets, fresh or frozen
⅓ cup French dressing
3 large, firm tomatoes
1 can (1 pound) whole potatoes, drained

1½ teaspoons salt
  Dash pepper
1⅓ cup melted fat or oil

Thaw frozen wings or fillets. Skin wings and cut into strips approximately 1 inch wide by 4 inches long. Place fish in a shallow baking dish. Pour dressing over fish and let stand for 30 minutes. Wash tomatoes. Remove stem ends and cut into sixths. Remove fish, reserving dressing for basting. Roll wings and place on skewers alternately with tomatoes and potatoes until skewers are filled. Place kabobs in well-greased, hinged wire grills. Add salt, pepper, and remaining dressing to fat; mix thoroughly. Baste kabobs with seasoned fat. Cook about 4 inches from moderately hot coals for 4 to 6 minutes. Baste with sauce. Turn and cook for 4 to 6 minutes longer or until fish flakes easily when tested with a fork. Serves six.

The authors are: Mildred L. Townsend, Home Advisor, San Luis Obispo County, Christopher M. Dewees, Extension Marine Resources Specialist, UC Davis, Robert J. Price, Extension Seafood Technologist, UC Davis.
Marine Advisory Programs, University of California, Davis 95616

## SMOKED SHARK

The best species to use for a smoked product are the soupfin, thresher, leopard, angel and dog shark (pin back). The blue shark is best prepared as jerky due to the softer nature of the flesh. This recipe also works well with salmon.

1. Fillet about 4 pounds of shark and cut the pieces into chunks or strips about 1″ to 1½″ thick and 2″ to 3″ wide.
2. Prepare a brine of: 2 cups of well packed dark brown sugar, 2/3 cup of salt, 1 tablespoon seafood seasoning (optional), and 2 quarts of water. Mix well until salt and sugar are dissolved.
3. Soak shark chunks in brine overnight.
4. Remove shark from brine and rinse well with fresh water.
5. Place shark on a rack in a cool, shady, breezy place to dry for about one hour. A tan shiny skin, or pellicle, should form on the surface.
6. Smoke in a commercial or homemade smoker for 10-14 hours depending on outside temperatures. It takes longer to dry in cold weather. The temperatures of the smoker should be between 130° and 150° F.
7. Wrap each piece of fish in heavy waxed paper. Some moisture is left in the smoked

product, so it should be refrigerated. Smoked shark should last two weeks or more, longer if frozen.

### SHARK JERKY

All sharks can be made into jerky, but the blue shark is especially good prepared in this way. Most other fish, as well as beef and deer, can also be made into jerky.

1. Fillet shark or fish and cut into strips approximately ¼″ to ½″ thick and 2″ wide. Use any length you desire. Cut across the grain of the muscle for a more tender product. Placing the shark in the freezer for a day or so makes slicing easier.
2. If the fish is frozen, thaw it and drain off the excess water.
3. For every 2 pounds of sliced shark or fish, prepare a sauce from: ⅛ cup teriyaki sauce, ⅛ cup liquid smoke, 6 drops of tabasco sauce, and one tablespoon of salt.
4. Place about ½ of prepared shark in a plastic bag. Pour ½ of sauce over shark. Add remaining shark and sauce. Roll bag back and forth to insure that the sauce covers all of the shark. The salt and sauce will make its own brine which will preserve the meat if all the air is expelled from the bag.
5. Marinate in the refrigerator for 8 hours (for blue shark) or 12 to 15 hours for other shark.

6. Remove marinated strips from refrigerator and place on ½″ square hardware cloth or other racks. Sprinkle garlic powder, onion powder, and coarse ground black pepper on both sides of strips.
7. Place racks in oven and set the oven to 140° F. A small smoker will also work well.
8. Blue shark should be dried about 12 hours. Other species may take less time. The time in the smoker will depend a great deal upon the amount of moisture in the flesh at the beginning of the process and the temperature of the smoker. Check at regular intervals and remove the fish before it becomes too dry.
   The finished product should be firm, dry and tough, yet not dry enough to crumble to the touch. When chewed, there should be some resiliency or rubbery characteristic to the meat. Overcooked jerky comes out crunchy.
9. The finished jerky should be stored in air-tight jars in a cool place.
10. The same methods can be used to make jerky from beef or deer. Remove all fat from beef or deer meat before cutting it into strips. Marinate the strips for 24 hours and dry for about 24 hours.

Prepared By:
John B. Richards, Area Marine Advisor, San
Luis Obispo, Santa Barbara and Ventura
Counties; Robert J. Price, Extension Seafood
Technology Specialist, University of
California, Davis.
Special thanks to Joe and Vonnie Pak of
Depoe Bay, Oregon for smoking recipe, and
Jim Graybill of Sandy, Oregon for sharing
the jerky recipe.
Marine Advisory Programs, University of
California, Davis, California 95616
(916) 752-1497   (916) 752-2193

## SILVERSIDES

At least half the fish sold as fresh smelt in
California markets are jacksmelt. Another 25
percent may be topsmelt. These are not true
smelt but members of the silverside family,
*Atherinidae*. Both jacksmelt and topsmelt
abound in the lower bay and provide year
round angling for the younger set who favor
light spinning outfits to catch these sporty
school fish.

### IDENTIFICATION
Jacksmelt and topsmelt have two dorsal fins,
whereas true smelt of the family *Osmeridae*
have only one dorsal fin. The latter fish are
caught mostly in the surf with beach seines or
triangular dip nets of a type used for centuries
by the Coast Indians.

Jacksmelt have bands of unforked teeth in the
jaws. There are at least ten rows of scales between the two dorsal fins.

Topsmelt have a single row of forked teeth and
no more than six rows of scales between the
dorsal fins.

### JACKSMELT
Jacksmelt have been reported to 22 inches in
length. Most caught from piers run less than 14
inches. During the spawning season that extends from October to March, jacksmelt
deposit millions of tiny eggs on seaweed in the
shallows. The fish are most numerous in the
Bay from January to April.

A school of jacksmelt is apt to turn up off a
pier on an incoming tide and leave when the
tide recedes. Since the schools travel at inter-
mediate depths, often two to four feet below
the surface, very few jacksmelt are caught on
tackle rigged for bottom fishing. The trick is to
determine the level where a school is
congregated and then fix a cork bobber or

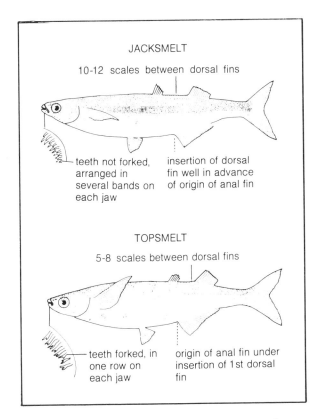

JACKSMELT

10-12 scales between dorsal fins

teeth not forked, arranged in several bands on each jaw

insertion of dorsal fin well in advance of origin of anal fin

TOPSMELT

5-8 scales between dorsal fins

teeth forked, in one row on each jaw

origin of anal fin under insertion of 1st dorsal fin

TOPSMELT

Topsmelt often school in company with a school of jacksmelt. Hooks as small as No. 16 are used for topsmelt, which average six or seven inches in length and rarely grow longer than a foot. As the name suggests, topsmelt tend to school very near the surface.

Both jacksmelt and topsmelt are very game fish, capable of some flashy pyrotechnics when hooked on light tackle. A fly rod with an enclosed-type spinning reel may be used where wind and water conditions permit use of a single split shot to sink the bait.

COOKING SUGGESTIONS

Topsmelt and small jacksmelt are usually dressed for pan frying the same as freshwater trout. Large jacksmelt may be filleted. Small parasites appearing as tiny "coiled-up worms" may be found in the flesh of jacksmelt. The Fish and Game Department advises that these are harmless to man, if the fish is thoroughly cooked.

The following instructions for the preparation of smelt tempura come from a book of favorite recipes compiled by the Junior Matrons of the San Mateo Buddhist Temple.

plastic float on the line to hold the bait at this depth. Hooks no larger than size No. 4 are used, baited with scraps of clam, mussel, pile worm, or anchovy.

### SMELT TEMPURA

Wash smelt and press the back to loosen the bone. Remove head and slit on the back side up to the bone. Remove the bone and clean the fish. Sprinkle lightly with salt. Dip in Tempura Batter and fry.

### TEMPURA BATTER

1½ cups of flour
1 cup of water (approximately)
1 egg

Measure flour in bowl and add cold water. With chopsticks, stir slightly until the flour is lumpy. Too much mixing will cause the batter to become doughy. Add unbeaten egg to the flour and stir lightly until egg is broken, but do not mix too well. The batter should be soft, but not smooth. Two eggs may be used if preferred.

### TEMPURA FRYING

Using an electric fryer, Dutch oven, or any deep iron frying pan, add salad oil until the pan is approximately 3/4 full. Mazola or Wesson oil is recommended. The oil should be hot enough so that, when tested with a little drop of batter, the batter sizzles and floats. Always keep oil at even temperature and, as the oil decreases after frying, add new oil to keep the frying pan 3/4 full.

Cook Book Committee, Junior Matrons of the San Mateo Buddhist Temple.

## STRIPED BASS

On San Francisco Bay and adjoining waterways of the Sacramento-San Joaquin River Delta is concentrated one of the most diversified sport fisheries in North America. The Delta complements the Bay with such freshwater game species as crappie, catfish, and black bass, as well as migratory salmon, sturgeon, and shad. But the mainstay of both Bay and Delta angling is "old linesides" of the family *Serranidae*, otherwise known as the striped bass.

Striped bass were not found anywhere in Western waters before 1879. In that year, the pioneer fish culturist, Livingston Stone, released to the Bay at Martinez 132 young stripers transported by rail from New Jersey. A few hundred more bass were stocked in 1882 but this plant was probably redundant. Just ten years after the first plant, locally caught stripers became available in San Francisco fish markets.

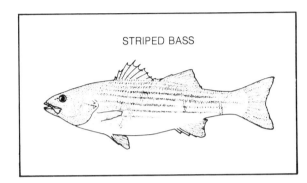

STRIPED BASS

Presently, the Fish and Game Department estimates that each year about 200,000 anglers catch a quarter million striped bass. The bass average from five to ten pounds and range to fifty-five pounds in weight. Anglers take them by trolling, casting, and still fishing in all kinds of water from quiet Delta sloughs to the raging surf off beaches near the Golden Gate.

Striped bass are anadromous fish which make regular migrations between the saltwater of the Bay and ocean and the freshwater of the Delta. The migrations are not precisely timed but, in recent years, the main movement of bass to fresh and brackish water has taken place during October and November. During winter, the large adult fish may be scattered from upper San Pablo Bay through the Delta waterways.

Spawning takes place in the Delta in April, May, and June. Through summer, impressive numbers of bass are caught on the lower bay and coastal waters off the Gate by anglers fishing from skiffs, cruisers, and sport fishing partyboats.

IDENTIFICATION

Striped bass are spiny-rayed fish with two dorsal fins. The caudal fin is notched. The fish are colored olive green to steel blue on top, the belly is white, and there are seven or eight dark horizontal stripes on the sides.

The record striped bass caught with hook and line in California weighed 65 pounds. Before commercial fishing for stripers was outlawed, a San Francisco fish market reported delivery of a 78-pound bass.

ANGLING

Most catches of striped bass from piers are made incidentally by anglers fishing primarily for perch, flounder, or other species. Often, a school of hungry stripers will chase bait fish to the vicinity of a pier, but such runs are sporadic and unpredictable. A large mature striper wandering apart from a school may turn up at any pier at any time of year. So the regulars nearly always use tackle suitable for taking a bass regardless of what kind of fish they expect to catch. This might be a conventional free-spool outfit or saltwater spinning gear with enough backbone for casting sinkers to five ounces.

Long rods to nine feet are favored, even though they are awkward to use on a crowded pier. The long rod provides the angler who has hooked a big strong fish a better chance to steer his catch away from the pilings or his neighbor's line.

Probably night fishing with live bait offers the best chance of success on a pier for anglers only interested in catching bass. Stripers are prone to feed heavily at night. A live shiner perch or mudsucker often proves irresistible to "old linesides" when other offerings fail.

COOKING SUGGESTIONS

Striped bass are among the most prized foodfish in the Bay. As steaks they may be barbecued. As fillets they may be baked, boiled, broiled, pan fried, or prepared in the Japanese style to be eaten raw. Here is a favorite recipe from the pages of the Fish and Game Department's monthly magazine, *Outdoor California*.

CIOPPINO

2 pounds fish fillet
1 cup water
1 finely chopped yellow onion
1 finely chopped garlic clove
1 tablespoon Worcestershire sauce
¼ teaspoon hot mustard
1 tablespoon butter
1 medium can stewed tomatoes
1 small can tomato paste
1 teaspoon chopped parsley
1 dollop red wine
1 dash Tabasco
  juice of one-half lemon
  salt and pepper to taste

Heat the finely chopped onion in the butter until golden brown. Be careful not to let the onion burn. Add the parsley and garlic, mix well, and let these tastes argue gently in a warm pan while you chop the tomatoes, then mix all other ingredients in your cooking pot. Add the fish after all other ingredients have mixed thoroughly. Cook over moderate heat for about 25 minutes, or until the fish meat is a creamy white. Keep your stirring to a minimum as it tends to flake the fish. Serve in bowls with plenty of French sourdough bread and butter.

Be sure you use a firm solid fish for this recipe,

perhaps striped bass, rockfish, or sole. Unless you want a flaky cioppino.

From Chef Quin's Game Gourmet column in *Outdoor California*

## STURGEON

Relatively few sturgeon caught in San Francisco Bay are taken from piers. Most of the sport catch is accounted for by partyboats and skiff fishermen. Still, the chance, however slight, of hooking one of the world's largest fish should lend excitement if not a touch of glamour to any pier fishing excursion.

Sturgeon, the source of caviar that presently retails for about $10 an ounce, is a very primitive fish with a largely cartilaginous skeleton. Some kinds of sturgeon are found only in freshwater. Those in the Bay are anadromous fish which migrate up rivers to spawn. The world record for a sturgeon taken with hook and line was established by W. H. McNew when he caught a 405-pound sturgeon at the mouth of the Feather River near Verona, California, in 1972.

In recent years, several sturgeon scaling better than 300 pounds have been reported taken by

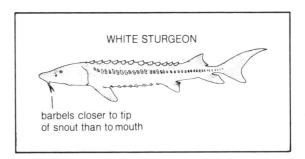

WHITE STURGEON

barbels closer to tip of snout than to mouth

skiff fishermen on San Pablo Bay. But, as sturgeon grow, these were not bragging size. Chinese laborers, returning from the mines at the tag end of the Gold Rush, snagged sturgeon in Delta waters that weighed over 1,000 pounds and measured up to thirteen feet in length. In the Caspian Sea, commercial fishermen trap beluga sturgeon that weigh close to a ton.

Two species of the sturgeon family, *Acipenseridae*, dwell in San Francisco Bay. Most common is the white sturgeon which roams the entire Bay but is particularly abundant in upper San Pablo Bay and Suisun Bay. The green sturgeon is a smaller fish which seems more oriented to the outer coast. It migrates up several North Coast rivers, including the Eel and Klamath.

## IDENTIFICATION

The body of a sturgeon is long and cylindrical. The mouth is sucker-like (no teeth) and there are four barbels on the underside of the snout. The skin is smooth but lined with rows of bony plates that have sharp spines. The white sturgeon is colored grey whereas the green sturgeon is olive green with a greenish stripe on each side.

## ANGLING

Intensive commercial fishing in the late 1800's led to a rapid decline in the numbers of white sturgeon. It was claimed the fish were on the verge of extinction when the California legislature put an end to sturgeon fishing in 1917.

Sturgeon may live to be 100 years old but are very slow-growing. So when the fishery was reopened in 1954, only sport fishing was permitted with a bag limit of one fish per day. At first, the minimum size was set at 50 inches. Later, this was reduced to 40 inches.

But ten years went by before Bay anglers found a way to fish for sturgeon. For all of 1962, only one sturgeon was reported caught by the partyboat fleet. A few individuals kept experimenting with various baits and angling techniques until finally a veteran partyboat skipper named Johnny Severa discovered that sturgeon have a weakness for grass shrimp. In 1965, the partyboat catch shot up to 1,731 sturgeon.

Catching sturgeon off piers is a more recent development not likely to become popular because of the great amount of patience, know-how, and physical endurance this fishing requires. Presently, only a handful of regulars who frequent North Bay piers deliberately fish for sturgeon. Any man, woman, or child bottom fishing from a pier may chance to hook a sturgeon, but the odds are poor the fish will remain on the line for more than a few seconds. When playing a hooked sturgeon, the skiff fisherman enjoys the advantage of greater mobility. He may sit back and let the fish tow him around the Bay until it runs out of gas.

Sturgeon are very stubborn fighters not prone to cease resistance until completely exhausted. There have been many instances of pier fishermen playing a big sturgeon for three to five hours only to lose the fish by attempting to gaff it prematurely. Yet, despite the difficulties almost every week at least one respectable-sized sturgeon is reported caught from some pier on the Bay.

The extra heavy tackle some of the old timers use for sturgeon is not favored on the piers. The regulars mostly employ the same rod and reel combination used for striped bass with 20 to 30 pound test line. The terminal tackle is rigged for bottom fishing with size No. 1/0 to 5/0 hooks, depending on the size of the bait which may be grass shrimp, ghost shrimp, or a live mudsucker.

In place of a weight at the end of the leader, some anglers prefer to use a sliding sinker because sturgeon will reject a bait if they sense the least bit of resistance. When a sturgeon takes an angler's offering, there may be no more than a gentle tap on the line, the same as when a flounder bites. Some experts say the rod should be struck when a second tap is felt. Others believe it's better to wait until the sturgeon begins taking line.

COOKING SUGGESTIONS

Sturgeon are fat fish, so rich they may be roasted as well as baked, broiled, or pan fried. A favorite dish in the Bay Area is barbecued sturgeon steaks. One party boat captain recommends barbecuing the steaks for four minutes on each side after they have been marinated for 24 hours in olive oil containing onions, garlic, and parsley.

Detailed instructions on how to make caviar at home are contained in A. J. McClane's *Standard Fishing Encyclopedia*. The Fish and Game Department advises that eggs to be used as caviar should be taken about April before they become ripe.

When cleaning a sturgeon, care should be taken to avoid cutting the notochord, a smooth rod-like structure that runs lengthwise through the backbone. The notochord contains a bitter substance that can detract from the flavor of the fish. However, marine biologist Donald Fry advises that, if the notochord is cut accidentally, a quick rinse should take care of the problem.

## SURFPERCH

The saltwater pan fish commonly known in the Bay Area as perch are not true perch. Ichthyologists classify these spiny-rayed fish as members of the surfperch family for which the scientific name is *Embiotocidae*.

Surfperch are unique to coastal waters from Baja California to Alaska. The true perch of the family *Percidae* are an exclusively freshwater group of fish not native to lakes and streams west of the Rockies.

Some kinds of surfperch which frequent reefs and rocky tidepools on the outer coast are rarely caught from piers. There is a surfperch which remains offshore in deep water and another that resides in the freshwater of the Sacramento-San Joaquin River Delta. Of the twenty known species of surfperch, about seven or eight contribute heavily to the sport catch inside the Golden Gate.

## IDENTIFICATION

Surfperch have oval or oblong bodies with up to eleven sharp spines in the dorsal fin. Three spines and thirteen or more soft rays are present in the anal fin. Most kinds of surfperch are silvery overall although some, including the black, striped, and rainbow surfperches, are brightly colored and others, such as the rubberlip perch, have dark sides.

## ANGLING

Surfperch are voracious feeders which travel about in schools on an unending quest for food. The schools often turn up off piers on a running tide to forage on little crabs and other crustaceans that dwell around pilings.

When hooked on light tackle, a surfperch may be counted on to put up a terrific fight for its size. This fish is notorious for sudden lunges and short lightning-fast runs which may serve to dislodge the hook. While playing a wildly gyrating perch, the angler must strive to keep the line away from the pier where it may fray and break against a barnacle-encrusted piling.

Angling technique and the manner in which the terminal tackle is rigged depend on water conditions and the depth where the perch are concentrated. Redtail and rubberlip perch often forage along the bottom. Calico and walleye tend to favor depths midway to the bottom. Shiner perch usually school near the surface. Hook sizes Nos. 4 and 6 are used for large perch. Popular baits include shrimp, mussels, pile worms, blood worms, tiny rock crabs, and strips of anchovy.

In their enthusiasm to attack a bait, wee shiner perch often hook themselves. Large perch may begin by nibbling or gently mouthing the offering. Should the angler try to set the hook, the fish will back off and swim away. Usually, it's best to wait until the perch begins taking line before striking the rod.

## REDTAIL SURFPERCH

From December through April on San Francisco Bay, the redtail surfperch shares top billing with the starry flounder as the game species most sought after by pier fishermen. In these months, both fish frequent shallow waters close to shore—the flounder to lay eggs and the redtail perch to give birth to live young.

Redtail perch are silvery in appearance with nine to eleven vertical bronze, brown, or orange bars along the sides. The tail and pelvic fins are usually tinged with red. The females of the species may attain sixteen inches in length.

Close cousins of the redtail perch are the calico and barred surfperches. Both are caught in the Bay but are more abundant farther down the coast. The sides of the barred surfperch are lined with brassy olive spots and vertical bars. It is the leading game fish taken in the surf off Southern California beaches. Calico surfperch have a soup plate configuration and silvery sides speckled with reddish brown markings.

WALLEYE SURFPERCH

The walleye is an important sport and commercial species which grows to nine inches in length. It has very large eyes, faint vertical bars on silvery sides, and black-tipped pelvic fins. The spotfin and silver surfperches are almost identical in appearance except their pelvic fins are not tipped with black. The spotfin usually has a touch of black on the anal fin.

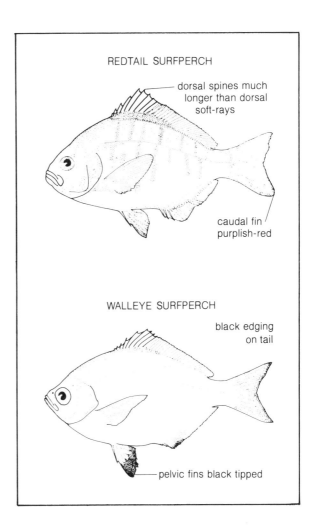

REDTAIL SURFPERCH

dorsal spines much longer than dorsal soft-rays

caudal fin purplish-red

WALLEYE SURFPERCH

black edging on tail

pelvic fins black tipped

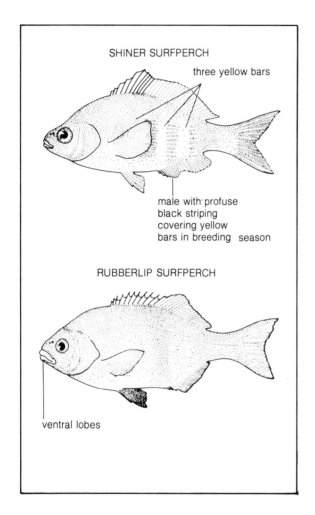

SHINER SURFPERCH

three yellow bars

male with profuse
black striping
covering yellow
bars in breeding  season

RUBBERLIP SURFPERCH

ventral lobes

### SHINER PERCH

Shiner perch rarely exceed six inches in length. A hook as small as size No. 10 is used to catch this scrappy little fish that will seek to devour most any natural bait that is smaller than itself.

Shiner perch are tinged with green on top with eight horizontal sooty lines on their silvery sides. Behind the pectoral fin are three vertical lemon yellow bars which suggest the figure 711. In breeding season, the males turn dark and acquire a black spot on either side of the snout.

A publication of the California Fish and Game Department says, "Probably more shiner perch are carted home by proud youngsters and furtively discarded by not-so-proud mothers than any other California marine fish."

### RUBBERLIP PERCH

The rubberlip perch is highly rated as a food fish and grows the largest of any surfperch in the Bay. It has been reported in lengths to eighteen inches. This perch does not appear to be overly abundant inside the Golden Gate but is seen frequently in catches made off the piers at Berkeley and Emeryville.

As the name suggests, the rubberlip perch has large lips, which may be white or pink. The sides have a coppery hue. The pelvic, dorsal, and anal fins are dusky and sometimes tipped with black.

### WHITE SEAPERCH
The white seaperch is also known as the splittail perch because its tail fin is deeply forked. It is a leading commercial species that grows to a foot in length. The fish is silvery overall, sometimes with a dusky or rosy orange cast. A dark line runs along the base of the dorsal fin.

### PILE PERCH
Splittail is also an alternate name for the pile perch. The tail is forked but this fish is easy to tell apart from the white seaperch because the first soft ray on the dorsal fin is twice as tall as the last dorsal spine. Pile perch attain lengths up to sixteen inches.

### BLACK SURFPERCH
Black surfperch are most abundant in Southern California but some are caught off piers, jetties, and seawalls on the lower bay and outer coast. The name is something of a misnomer because the black surfperch is one of the most brightly colored surfperches.

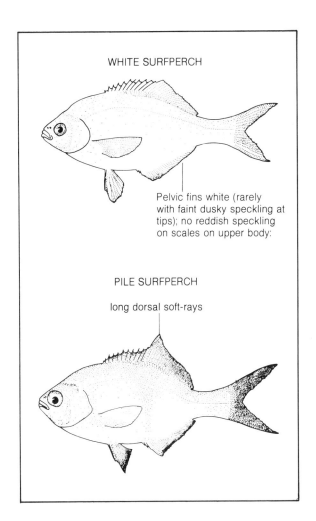

WHITE SURFPERCH

Pelvic fins white (rarely with faint dusky speckling at tips); no reddish speckling on scales on upper body:

PILE SURFPERCH

long dorsal soft-rays

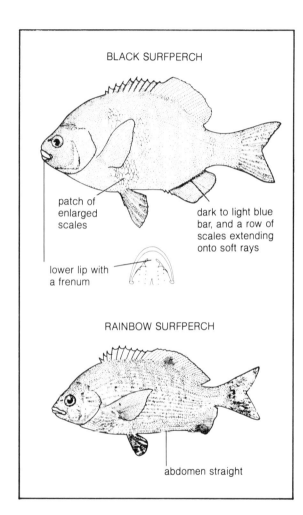

BLACK SURFPERCH

patch of
enlarged
scales

dark to light blue
bar, and a row of
scales extending
onto soft rays

lower lip with
a frenum

RAINBOW SURFPERCH

abdomen straight

Black surfperch caught late in the year sometimes appear jet black. More often, these fish are predominately brown, blue, or orange with a sprinkling of other vivid hues. The sides are scored with nine dark vertical bars. The lips may be yellow or an orangy brown.

The black surfperch is an excellent foodfish. It rarely exceeds fourteen inches in length but tends to grow plumper than other surfperches.

RAINBOW SEAPERCH
The sides of the rainbow seaperch are lined horizontally with red, orange, and blue stripes. Streaks of orange and blue appear on the head and the fins are brightly colored.

The rainbow surfperch frequents rocky shores on the outer coast. A few are taken off the jetties at Half Moon Bay.

STRIPED SEAPERCH
Striped seaperch are mainly caught off the outer coast but some are hooked by anglers who fish the seawall at Fort Point. This handsome fish is striped horizontally with shades of dull orange and blue. Overall, the fish has a coppery hue.

COOKING SUGGESTIONS

Properly prepared, surfperch have a fine, delicate flavor. But since these are dry fish, it's important to avoid overcooking. The flesh is lean, close-grained, with less than five per cent fat.

Medium to large surfperch may be prepared as fillets. Small fish are gutted, scaled, and beheaded. The whole fish or fillets may be rolled in seasoned flour and cooked quickly in deep fat.

For pan frying, the fillets are dipped in egg and breaded with fine crumbs. Cook over fairly high heat, allowing no more than two minutes for each side. Prior to cooking, the flavor may be enhanced by marinating the fillets for a few hours in a French dressing made with lemon juice.

Sooner or later, the cook in every family that includes one or more pier fishermen faces the dilemma of preparing an odd assortment of fish for the table. For example, the day's catch might include several varieties of surfperch, a couple of jacksmelt, a small flounder, a medium-size kingfish, and perhaps a tomcod or two.

One way to cope with this mess of fish is to convert them into fish cakes. The following recipe comes from Chef Quin's Game Gourmet column which regularly appears in *Outdoor California*, a publication of the California Fish and Game Department.

BAKED FISH BALLS

| 2 | eggs |
|---|---|
| 4 | onions |
| 3 | carrots |
| 4 | potatoes |
| 1 | cup hot water |
| 1 | tablespoon salt |
| 2 | teaspoons chopped parsley |
| 3 | tablespoons cracker meal |
| 3 | tablespoons shortening |
| 1 | teaspoon white pepper |
| 3 | tablespoons butter |
| 3½ | pounds assorted fish |

First, bone the fish, cutting the meat into small pieces. Put the meat through a grinder along with two onions, cracker meal, and seasonings. Repeat this operation until the combination is well mixed and you have a fine mixture. When this is done, add the eggs and again mix the ingredients thoroughly.

Next grease a large baking dish with the shortening. Cut both the carrots and the potatoes into strips about a quarter of an inch thick. Slice the two remaining onions as thin as possible. Line the bottom of the dish with layers of onion, carrot, and potato.

Shape the fish mixture into balls and place them on the vegetables. Pour hot water over the ingredients and top each ball with a small portion of butter.

Bake the dish in a moderate oven, about 300 degrees, for an hour and a half. Serve hot with your favorite relish, or you can make a light milk gravy. A cottage cheese, peach, and lettuce salad and ginger snap cookies round out a great meal.

Also, there is nothing in my recipe which says you have to use only rockfish or freshwater fish for these balls. This is one of the times when a combination of the two can be pretty tasty.

The Game Gourmet with Chef Quin,
*Outdoor California*

# POTPOURRI

Anglers who fish from piers on the Bay or ocean can never be sure what may turn up at the end of their lines. Not infrequently, crabs are hooked. Among the unusual catches reported by anglers at Pacifica Pier are starfish, baby octopuses, and giant sea snails. Recently, a man casting from the old ferry pier at Martinez hooked a 24-inch steelhead rainbow trout.

The fish listed below may be caught at some Bay Area piers but normally account for only a small fraction of the annual catch.

### PACIFIC JACK MACKEREL
Jack mackerel are not true mackerel but a close relative of the California yellowtail, a game fish much sought after in the ocean off San Diego. Both fish are members of the jack family, *Carangidae.* Jack mackerel school near the surface and may range as far as 600 miles out to sea. They may live for thirty years but the largest on record barely exceeded five pounds in weight. Jack mackerel occasionally show up off Bay piers at which time they may be receptive to cut bait.

A superior foodfish, jack mackerel are best when broiled, barbecued, smoked, or fried in deep fat. To prepare for frying, the fish are skinned and filleted. Next, a strip of dark oily meat that runs along the sides is removed. Then the fillets may be dipped in egg or batter and rolled in seasoned bread crumbs.

PACIFIC HERRING

Each winter, some time in January, February, or March, a spawning run of Pacific herring creates pandemonium on the Sausalito waterfront. The arrival of the herring on an incoming tide is signaled by hordes of gulls, grebes, cormorants, and other fish-eating birds. Within minutes after the birds are sighted off a pier or seawall, the fisherman's grapevine draws a crowd of men, women, and children armed with dip nets of half-inch mesh.

The technique employed for dip netting is primitive but effective. The net is lowered into the water with a rope. When herring are felt bumping the net, it is swiftly retrieved and the catch of eight- to eleven-inch fish are poured into a tub. Usually, a few herring are retained for pan frying the same as trout. The rest of the catch may be pickled, salted, smoked, or frozen.

Pacific herring belong to the same family, *Clupeidae*, as the Pacific sardine and American white shad. Female herring produce up to 40,000 eggs, each the size of a pin head. During a run, the eggs are deposited in layers an inch thick on rocks and pilings near shore. Herring are sought by commercial fishermen mainly for their roe which is considered a delicacy in Japan.

Herring runs may last for several days or be confined to a single tide. After a run has peaked and the fish are too scarce for netting, anglers catch them with light freshwater

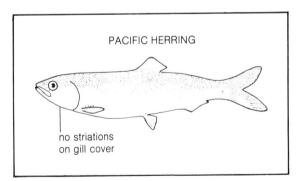

PACIFIC HERRING

no striations
on gill cover

tackle. Herring won't take bait but these sporty fish will often strike a shrimp fly tied on a No. 6 hook with a touch of red or yellow yarn.

One other place on the Bay where herring runs occur inshore is the old Parr Terminal Wharf at the tip of Point Richmond. This used to be a good fishing spot but now the pier is full of holes, fenced off, and posted with No Trespassing signs.

### TROUT AND SALMON

King salmon, silver salmon, and steelhead rainbow trout of the family *Salmonidae* are anadromous fish which spend most of their lives in the ocean but ascend rivers to propagate. These superb game fish play a very minor role in the pier fishery.

Once in a blue moon, someone is lucky enough to hook a steelhead from a pier on the North Bay. The only pier where salmon are caught in significant numbers is at Pacifica.

During the saltwater phase of their existence, king salmon, silver salmon, and steelhead all tend to look alike—blue or bluish on top with bright silvery sides. One way to tell them apart is to inspect the mouth. The mouth of a steelhead is white inside, the king salmon's is

dark, the silver salmon has a dark mouth with white gums around the teeth.

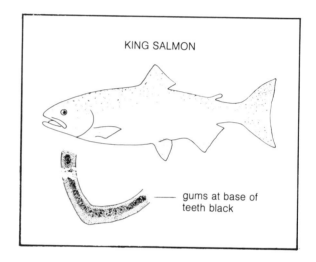

KING SALMON

gums at base of teeth black

TOMCOD

The little tomcod of the cod family *Gadidae* is the only true cod found in any abundance off the California coast. It rarely attains a foot in length and has no commercial importance.

Tomcods are not rare off Bay piers. But neither are they sufficiently numerous and easy to catch to command much interest from the younger set. Tomcod are the only fish commonly found in the Bay that have three separate dorsal fins and a barbel under the lower jaw. For more on tomcod, see the pages on Muni Pier.

ROCKFISH

The term rockfish is used in two ways. Rockfish is the official common name for the more than fifty different species of spiny-rayed fish that belong to the rockfish family, *Scorpaenidae*. The latter, which come in many different color schemes, are commonly spoken of as rock cod but are not closely related to cod. Fillets of rockfish are sold in fish markets as rock cod or red snapper.

Also the term rockfish is widely used in referring to all kinds of fish that frequent coastal waters where the bottom is rocky. Examples are lingcod, cabezon, and kelp greenling which are also known as greenling seatrout.

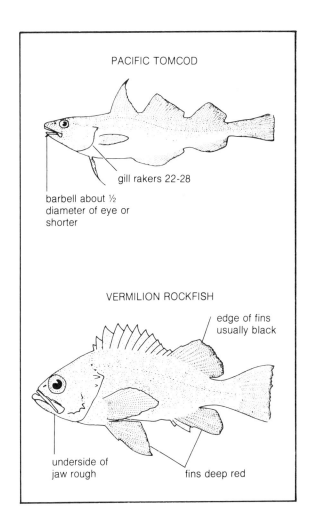

PACIFIC TOMCOD

gill rakers 22-28

barbell about ½ diameter of eye or shorter

VERMILION ROCKFISH

edge of fins usually black

underside of jaw rough

fins deep red

Relatively few rockfish are caught from piers in the Bay Area because most are located where the bottom is mud or sand. The places mentioned in this book where rockfish may be hooked include the Muni Pier, the seawall at Fort Point, and the jetties at Pillar Point Harbor on Half Moon Bay. Large numbers of rockfish are taken by sports fishing partyboats which operate from Pillar Point Harbor. Here is a recipe recommended for rockfish by Captain Walt of the Pillar Point Fishing Trips.

CRISPY FISH WITH SWEET AND SOUR SAUCE
Make a running batter of ¼ cup flour, ¼ cup cornstarch, salt to taste, and ½ cup of water. Cut one pound rock cod fillets into 1½-inch squares. Salt and let stand for twenty minutes. Dip in batter and deep fry until brown. Place on platter. Boil together five tablespoons brown sugar, four tablespoons vinegar or lemon juice, two tablespoons of ketchup, two teaspoons of soy sauce, ½ teaspoon of sesame oil, one cup of water, two slices of crushed ginger, two cloves of crushed garlic. Add cornstarch if necessary to thicken. Pour hot over platter of fish. Garnish with sweet or sour pickles.

# V
# How to Prepare and Cook Your Catch

SCALING

Wash the fish. Place the fish on a cutting board and with one hand hold the fish firmly by the head. Holding a knife almost vertical, scrape off the scales, starting at the tail and scraping toward the head. Be sure to remove all the scales around the fins and head.

CLEANING

With a sharp knife cut the entire length of the belly from the vent to the head. Remove the intestines. Next, cut around the pelvic fins and remove them.

REMOVING THE HEAD AND TAIL

Remove the head and the pectoral fins by cutting just back of the collarbone. If the backbone is large, cut down to it on each side of the fish.

Then place the fish on the edge of the cutting board so that the head hangs over and snap the backbone by bending the head down. Cut any remaining flesh that holds the head to the body. Cut off the tail.

REMOVING THE FINS

Next remove the dorsal fin, the large fin on the back of the fish, by cutting along each side of the fin. Then give a quick pull forward toward the head and remove the fin with the root bones attached. Remove the ventral fin in the same way. Never trim the fins off with shears or a knife because the root bones at the base of the fins will be left in the fish. Wash the fish thoroughly in cold running water. The fish is now dressed or pan-dressed, depending on its size.

CUTTING STEAKS

Large size dressed fish may be cut crosswise into steaks, about an inch thick.

FILLETING

With a sharp knife cut along the back of the fish from the tail to the head. Then cut down to the backbone just back of the collarbone.

Turn the knife flat and cut the flesh away from the backbone and rib bones.

Lift off the whole side of the fish or fillet in one piece. Turn the fish over and cut the fillet from the other side.

SKINNING A FILLET

If you wish, you may skin the fillets. Place the fillet, skin side down, on a cutting board. Hold the tail end tightly with your fingers and with a sharp knife cut down through the flesh to the skin about ½ inch from the end of the fillet. Flatten the knife against the skin and cut the flesh away from the skin by sliding the knife forward while holding the tail end of the skin firmly between your fingers.

*From Let's Cook Fish! A Complete Guide to Fish Cookery,* Department of Commerce, National Marine Fisheries Service, Washington, D. C. 20240

## TIMETABLE FOR COOKING FISH

| Method of Cooking | Market Form | Amount for 6 | Cooking Temp. | Approximate Cooking Time (minutes) |
|---|---|---|---|---|
| Baking | Dressed | 3 pounds | 350° F. | 45 to 60 |
| | Pan-dressed | 3 pounds | 350° F. | 25 to 30 |
| | Fillets or steaks | 2 pounds | 350° F. | 20 to 25 |
| | Frozen fried fish portions | 12 portions (2½ to 3 ounces each) | 400° F. | 15 to 20 |
| | Frozen fried fish sticks | 24 sticks (¾ to 1¼ ounces each) | 400° F. | 15 to 20 |

| Method of Cooking | Market Form | Amount for 6 | Cooking Temp. | Approximate Cooking Time (minutes) |
|---|---|---|---|---|
| Broiling | Pan-dressed | 3 pounds | | 10 to 16 (turning once) |
| | Fillets or steaks | 2 pounds | | 10 to 15 |
| | Frozen fried fish portions | 12 portions (2½ to 3 ounces each) | | 10 to 15 |
| | Frozen fried fish sticks | 24 sticks (¾ to 1¼ ounces each) | | 10 to 15 |
| Charcoal Broiling | Pan-dressed | 3 pounds | Moderate | 10 to 16 (turning once) |
| | Fillets or steaks | 2 pounds | Moderate | 10 to 16 (turning once) |
| | Frozen fried fish portions | 12 portions (2½ to 3 ounces each) | Moderate | 8 to 10 (turning once) |
| | Frozen fried fish sticks | 24 sticks (¾ to 1¼ ounces each) | Moderate | 8 to 10 (turning once) |
| Deep Fat Frying | Pan-dressed | 3 pounds | 350° F. | 3 to 5 |
| | Fillets or steaks | 2 pounds | 350° F. | 3 to 5 |
| | Frozen raw breaded fish portions | 12 portions (2½ to 3 ounces each) | 350° F. | 3 to 5 |
| Oven-Frying | Pan-dressed | 3 pounds | 500° F. | 15 to 20 |
| | Fillets or steaks | 2 pounds | 500° F. | 10 to 15 |
| Pan Frying | Pan-dressed | 3 pounds | Moderate | 8 to 10 (turning once) |
| | Fillets or steaks | 2 pounds | Moderate | 8 to 10 (turning once) |
| | Frozen raw breaded or frozen fried fish portions | 12 portions (2½ to 3 ounces each) | Moderate | 8 to 10 (turning once) |
| | Frozen fried fish sticks | 24 sticks (¾ to 1¼ ounces each) | Moderate | 8 to 10 (turning once) |
| Poaching | Fillets or steaks | 2 pounds | Simmer | 5 to 10 |
| Steaming | Fillets or steaks | 1½ pounds | Boil | 5 to 10 |

From *Let's Cook Fish! A Complete Guide to Fish Cookery*, Department of Commerce, National Marine Fisheries Service, Washington, D.C. 20240

**It Is Unlawful To...**
Take or possess Dungeness Crabs (Cancer magister) in all bay waters and tributaries east of the Golden Gate

(Sec. 29.85 Sport Fishing Regulations)

# VI
# Crabs

More than twenty species of crabs dwell in the Bay. Of these, only the rock crab, red crab, and Dungeness, or market crab, are valued for eating purposes. The Dungeness grows the largest and is most esteemed for its meat. However, *it is never legal to take Dungeness crabs from waters inside the Golden Gate.*

Both rock crabs and red crabs may be caught in the Bay at all times of the year with ring nets or similar devices. These crabs frequent the type of rock, sand, and gravel bottoms that exist off San Francisco's northern waterfront. Crabbing here is especially popular at the Fort Point, Fort Mason, Alcatraz, and Muni Piers.

| IDENTIFYING CRABS | | | |
|---|---|---|---|
| *Name* | *Carapace (back)* | *Claws* | *Maximum Size* |
| Red Crab *C. productus* | Dark to medium red | Black-tipped | Seven inches |
| Rock Crab *C. antennarius* | Dark to medium red | Black-tipped | Five inches |
| Dungeness or Market Crab *C. magister* | Reddish brown | White-tipped | Nine inches |

## IDENTIFICATION

Red, rock, and Dungeness crabs are closely related species of the genus Cancer and the family *Cancridae*. Dungeness crabs are easy to tell apart from rock crabs and red crabs because the latter have black-tipped claws whereas the claws of the Dungeness are white-tipped.

## CATCHING CRABS OFF PIERS

Crabbing with a ring net is easy to do. The ring or hoop net is a basket-type device attached by four short cords to the end of a rope. After a fish carcass or several fish heads are secured to the center of the net, it is tossed off the pier and allowed to rest flat on the bottom. Every ten minutes or so, the net is retrieved to see if a crab has been drawn to the bait.

If the catch is a red crab or rock crab, a measuring device is required to make certain the crab is of legal size. Regulations require that undersize rock crabs and red crabs, as well as Dungeness crabs of any size, be restored to the Bay.

In 1981, the minimum size for both rock and red crabs was four inches measured across the widest part of the back. The bag limit was 35 crabs.

Crabs should be kept alive before cooking in boiling water for ten to twenty minutes. The pot should contain enough water to cover the crabs, with two tablespoons of salt added for each quart of water.

The favorite creel for crabs used to be an old burlap sack soaked with sea water. Now that burlap sacks have become scarce, many of the regulars contain their catch in a tall bucket with some seaweed in it.

Most of the edible meat in rock crabs and red crabs is found in the claws. So some fishermen simply remove the claws and return the crabs to the sea. A Fish and Game Department brochure authored by two marine biologists says, "Unfortunately, this is not a good practice, in that the crab without pincers will most likely die. It cannot hold its food to eat, especially when competing with crabs which have their claws. There is good body meat inside the shell, so it is best to use the entire crab. If you don't want to use the body meat, either throw the entire crab back or at least give it half a chance by taking only one of its claws."

After cooking, the top shell, gills, and viscera of a crab are removed preliminary to extracting the meat with a small pointed knife. The meat in the claws is fairly easy to remove once the shells have been cracked with a wooden mallet.

Dungeness crabs, as well as rock and red crabs, may be taken from piers on the outer coast at Pacifica and Half Moon Bay during the open season that usually runs from mid-November through June. Current angling regulations may be consulted for the exact dates.

In 1981, the minimum size for Dungeness crabs was 6¼ inches measured across the back in front of the lateral spines. The bag limit was ten crabs.

MYSTERY OF THE DUNGENESS CRAB
It is normal wherever Dungeness crabs are taken commercially for the fishery to suffer a few bad seasons every eight to ten years. But the Golden Gate fishery has been in a state of decline for more than twenty years. From a high of nine million pounds in the 1956-57 season, crab landings at San Francisco have fallen to less than a million pounds. Presently, most of the Dungeness crabs sold at Fisherman's Wharf and markets around the Bay come from Eureka or ports in the Pacific Northwest.

When it became apparent that this decline was not a normal cyclical downturn, complaints were directed against the commercial fleet for over fishing. But the commercials rebutted that pollution was to blame. Some scientists speculated that pesticides or heavy metals in the water might have rendered the crab eggs more vulnerable to parasites.

The Fish and Game Department took the position that not enough was known about the life history of the Dungeness crab to make a judgement. In 1975, the Department assigned a team of marine biologists to conduct a 5½-year study of the crab. The results of the study were announced shortly before this book went to press.

When the study began, it was known that a female Dungeness crab produces from one to two million eggs. In January, the babies emerge as free-floating larvae known as *zoeae*. The tiny crab larvae drift about in the currents for three months before they begin to develop claws and sink to the bottom.

The study team found that half the crabs remain at sea while the other half enter the

Bay. It is believed the latter are drawn through the Golden Gate by tidal currents.

The young crabs in the Bay grow faster than those that remain outside the Golden Gate. But after a year, before they have attained a width in excess of four inches, these crabs rejoin their brothers and sisters out in the ocean.

The study team found no abnormal condition in the Bay which might explain why fewer adult crabs were being caught at sea. Instead, results of the study indicated that changes in the ocean outside the Bay were to blame.

It seems that, during the late 1950's, a shift in ocean currents caused water temperatures off the Central California coast to be warmer than normal. This phenomenon interested the study team because the decline in the crab catch began about the same time as the warm spell. Earlier periods of abnormally warm water temperatures never lasted more than two or three years. The warm spell first noted in 1957 has persisted without a break to the present time.

Scientists say the higher temperatures occur because the relatively warm Davidson current that flows north is more developed off the coast than usual. This current runs counter to the colder California current that flows south.

The Fish and Game study team found that much of the annual crab hatch off San Francisco is carried away by the Davidson current to another place in the ocean. Some of the young castaways eventually return to Golden Gate waters but the fate of the others remains a mystery.